Ivory Towers on Sand

The Failure of Middle Eastern Studies in America

Martin Kramer

THE WASHINGTON INSTITUTE FOR NEAR EAST POLICY

© The Washington Institute for Near East Policy, 2001

Published in 2001 in the United States of America by The Washington Institute for Near East Policy, 1828 L Street NW, Suite 1050, Washington, DC 20036.

Second printing, 2002, by The Washington Institute for Near East Policy.

Library of Congress Cataloging-in-Publication Data

Kramer, Martin S.
  Ivory towers on sand: the failure of Middle Eastern studies in America/
  Martin Kramer.
      p. cm.
  Includes bibliographical references and index.
  ISBN 0-944029-49-3
  1. Middle East—Study and teaching—United States. I. Title.

  DS61.9.U6 K73 2001

956'.071'073—dc21   2001046518
                                              CIP

Cover image © Corbis. Cover design by Alicia Gansz.

The Author

Martin Kramer is editor of the *Middle East Quarterly* and past director of the Moshe Dayan Center for Middle Eastern and African Studies at Tel Aviv University. His experience of Middle Eastern studies in the United States has been extensive. He earned his undergraduate and doctoral degrees from Princeton University, and another graduate degree from Columbia University. He has been a visiting professor at the University of Chicago, Cornell University, and Georgetown University. On two occasions, Dr. Kramer has been a fellow of the Woodrow Wilson International Center for Scholars in Washington. His authored and edited books include *Islam Assembled; Shi'ism, Resistance and Revolution; Middle Eastern Lives; Arab Awakening and Islamic Revival; The Islamism Debate;* and *The Jewish Discovery of Islam.*

Dr. Kramer was The Washington Institute's Ira Weiner Fellow in 1999, when he began researching and writing this monograph.

• • •

• • •

For media coverage and reviews of this monograph, as well as additional commentary by the author, visit http://www.ivorytowers.org

Table of Contents

To Sandy, Anat, Keren, and Adam, for all the absences

Acknowledgments

I wrote a third of this study at The Washington Institute for Near East Policy, a third at the Woodrow Wilson International Center for Scholars in Washington, and a third at the Moshe Dayan Center for Middle Eastern and African Studies, Tel Aviv University. Robert Satloff and Patrick Clawson at The Washington Institute, and Robert Litwak at the Wilson Center, encouraged me at every stage. Without time off from my directorial duties, this study would have languished in a drawer, and I am grateful for the confidence of my Washington friends.

I will not implicate my university-based colleagues who shared their thoughts with me on the state of Middle Eastern studies in America. Not only did they save me from error, but some also shared their personal files, where I found useful materials. I received a crash course in the complexities of Title VI, the U.S. Department of Education's program for area studies, from these kind persons: Richard D. Brecht and Thomas W. Gething of the National Foreign Language Center, who are conducting a Department-sponsored review of Title VI; and G. Edward McDermott, the Middle East program officer at the Department of Education.

The easy access I had to the Library of Congress through the Wilson Center proved crucial to several chapters, and I am indebted to librarian Janet Spikes for her guidance. I am grateful to two research assistants, Marie-Amélie George and James Perlin, who tracked down most of the sources for this study. Last but not least, I am beholden to Alicia Gansz, who performed the entire range of a publisher's duties with consummate professionalism.

Finally, given the subject matter and my approach to it, I feel obliged to underline the customary *mea culpa*, that only the author is responsible for the errors and opinions in this study. If there are errors, rest assured that no one else could have made them. As for the opinions, they are unmistakably my own.

Martin Kramer

Preface

In the days immediately following the heinous attacks on the World Trade Center and the Pentagon, the American media turned to Middle East "experts" for over-the-airwaves analysis of the motivation, rationale, and ideology of the perpetrators—and, at times, for advice on what the United States should do in response. Not since the Gulf War a decade ago had so many academics been brought before the cameras and the microphones. Some were insightful, informed, and informative. Many, however, were superficial, misguided, and wrong.

As Martin Kramer argues in this courageous and path-breaking examination of the state of his profession, America is ill served by the way in which the Middle East is studied and presented at institutions of higher education across the nation. The academic understanding of the Middle East is framed not by the realities of the region, but by the fads and fashions that have swept through the disciplines. Many practitioners are members of the "leftover left," infused with third worldist biases. Many of the academics who hail from the region are still caught up in the passion of its discredited causes. There is a widespread sympathy for Middle Eastern radicalism and an abiding suspicion of America's global role.

As Dr. Kramer demonstrates, these biases have produced a distorted perception of change in the Middle East. If one had read only the analyses of academics over the last two decades, one would have concluded that Islamic movements were moderate forces of democratization, and that "civil society" was about to sweep away authoritarian regimes. Looking back, it is clear that the Middle East has completely defied the paradigms that have dominated the field of Middle Eastern studies. Americans who have followed the Pied Pipers of the academy have been surprised time and again by the real Middle East.

The institutions of Middle Eastern studies—departments, centers, professional associations, grant committees—have become bastions of conformism, hostile to intellectual diversity. Advocates of other approaches have been pushed to the margins of the guild or out of academe altogether (often into the more open world of the think tanks). If this were not enough, the empire of error benefits from millions of dollars in federal subsidies, funneled through the Department of Education.

The Washington Institute is pleased to publish this book. Speaking truth to power has been the prime mission of the Institute from its inception. Indeed, when the Institute was founded sixteen years ago, one of its objectives was to provide an antidote to the fallacies of the reigning orthodoxies of Middle Eastern studies, some of which had spilled over into Washington.

We are especially proud to have commissioned Martin Kramer to undertake this study during his tenure as the Institute's Ira Weiner Fellow. As Dr. Kramer writes in his introduction, he is an "intimate stranger" to the American academic scene—a product and observer of American Middle East studies, but not a captive of them. More important, he is an accomplished scholar in his own right, recognized internationally for his ability to synthesize the experience of Muslims in the modern world. Few scholars are as universally respected—in America, Europe, and across the Middle East—as Martin Kramer.

In virtually all prefaces to Institute publications, we note that we present this work in the hope of informing the Washington policy community about an issue of critical importance to U.S. interests in the Middle East. This work is different. It is a veritable "consumer's report" for the busy policymaker who needs to know about current Middle East affairs. This study is not about any one issue; it is about how Washington should process the information it receives from academe on *all* issues. And its message is straightforward: *caveat emptor*—let the buyer beware. *Ivory Towers on Sand* surely stands out as one of the most important studies The Washington Institute has ever had the privilege to publish.

Fred S. Lafer
President

Michael Stein
Chairman

Introduction

Are Middle Eastern studies in America in trouble? To judge from the numbers, the answer would appear to be "no." The Middle East Studies Association, known as MESA and founded in 1966, has more than 2,600 members. Across the country, there is an abundance of course offerings on the Middle East, and some 125 universities and colleges offer degrees or other programs on the area. Academics generate an endless stream of books and journal articles. New journals have proliferated. So too have new professional associations devoted to individual countries and the advancement of Middle Eastern scholarship within specific disciplines. MESA boasts thirty-four affiliated organizations.

Each fall, MESA convenes an annual conference that surpasses any comparable gathering anywhere in the world. This conference meets every three years in Washington, in an effort to demonstrate the health of the field to the government that subsidizes it. And subsidies do flow. The U.S. Department of Education presently funds fourteen National Resource Centers for the Middle East, at leading public and private universities across the country (see the Appendix). It also funds nearly one hundred full-time and summer fellowships for students enrolled at these centers. Funding for these programs is at all-time highs. It would be easy to assemble figures demonstrating a gradual but steady increase in the quantitative inputs and outputs of Middle Eastern studies in America. If there is a crisis, it is not to be found in the numbers.

Yet deep in collected volumes and academic journals, far from the public eye, a different picture emerges. Jerrold Green, a senior political scientist at RAND who once directed the Middle East center at the University of Arizona, looked back at academe in 1994 and concluded that "the Middle East field is in a crisis within the broader discipline of political science."[1] In 1998, he took only one step back: "Although it may be extreme to talk about a field in crisis, it is fair to say that this is a field in some trouble."[2]

In 1996, James Bill, another noted political scientist at William and Mary, reached the same conclusion: "All is not well in the field of Middle East political studies in the United States. A review of the history of Middle East scholarship suggests we have learned disturbingly little after 50 years of heavy exertion." Many scholars were "severely lacking in the skills necessary to understand and explain Middle Eastern politics," while the few senior scholars "seldom fulfill their potential in providing original insights and in-depth understanding of Middle East political processes."[3]

By 1999, a similar admission came from a source at the very pinnacle of the field. "Few scholars of the Middle East are in a position to take much satisfaction in the disarray in post-Soviet studies," wrote Lisa Anderson, a political scientist and dean of international and public affairs at Columbia, "for we face dilemmas of comparable magnitude without even being fully aware of it. The end of the Cold War had its own particular dynamic in the Middle East and our failure to capture it is a measure of how little we understood its role in shaping politics in the region in the first place."[4] Admissions of failure in academe are rare occurrences, and are usually made only when the fact of failure is indisputable.

It could be argued, in response, that there is nothing new about this and that scholars have a natural proclivity for lamenting the state of their fields. But it has been a long time since scholars of the Middle East looked critically at themselves. In the 1970s, the field underwent a wrenching crisis, prompted by Middle Eastern turmoil, academic radicalization, and budget cutting. It ended in a great shakeout and a shift of academic power. The new leaders of the field claimed to be more competent, and prided themselves upon possession of more potent paradigms for explaining and understanding the Middle East. They would not make the mistakes of their predecessors. For more than twenty years they have interpreted and predicted Middle Eastern politics with a supreme confidence in their own powers.

Only now have hesitant voices been raised from within the ramparts, pointing to serious problems. They run even deeper than insiders are prepared to admit. It is no exaggeration to say that America's academics have failed to predict or explain the major evolutions of Middle Eastern politics and society over the past two decades. Time and again, academics have been taken by surprise by their subjects; time and again, their paradigms have been swept away by events. Repeated failures have depleted the credibility of scholarship among influential publics. In Washington, the mere mention of academic Middle Eastern studies often causes eyes to roll. The purpose of this paper is to probe how and why a branch of academe once regarded with esteem has descended to such a low point in the public estimate, and what might be done about it.

Chapter one considers just what constitutes Middle Eastern studies in their unique American configuration. Chapter two examines the crucial impact of Edward Said's *Orientalism*. Chapters three and four document and analyze the collective errors made by the academic experts in assessing Islamism and "civil society," two core issues that preoccupied the field in the 1990s. Chapter five examines the relevance gap that has opened up between academics and policymakers, and the alienation that besets both sides. Chapter six analyzes the loss of public, philanthropic, and academic confidence in Middle Eastern studies. The conclusion considers what might be done to find another way forward.

A few qualifications are in order. In American usage, many branches of scholarship fall under the rubric of "Middle Eastern studies," from Ottoman architecture to Arabic linguistics. Some of these branches have flourished, not failed. A truly reliable assessment of all aspects of Middle Eastern studies could only be accomplished by a multidisciplinary team. But scholars of modern history and contemporary politics enjoy the highest profile in the field. Their texts are assigned in large courses; they are interviewed and quoted; and, in most years, it is they who are elected presidents of MESA. This critique does not claim to encompass all of Middle Eastern studies. But it does accurately identify and aim for the representative center of the field, the points where leaders, ideas, and resources have come together to forge dominant paradigms. It is from these points that the field is defined and defended, and it is here that the trouble resides.

Second, it is important to remember that Islamism and "civil society" do not exhaust the issues that have concerned students of the modern and contemporary Middle East these past twenty years. In their reading of Iran and Arab-Israeli relations, academics again have diverged significantly from other loci of expertise. One observer has written of "a deep and widening gap between the perception of Iran by the Washington policy community, on the one hand, and by many if not most academic specialists on the other."[5] And largely as a result of Edward Said's influence, academics have tended to discount the "peace process" altogether.[6] It could be argued that, on both these issues, academe has failed or is failing. But the case would not be clear cut, because Iranian politics and Arab-Israeli relations still leave room for contradictory interpretations. Any critique of academic performance on these two issues must await a lengthening of perspective.

Third and last, it should not be assumed from this account that Middle Eastern studies cannot change. Indeed, were it not for a sense of impasse within the field itself, there would be no point in offering a critique. The day seems not far off when discontent might coalesce into a new agenda. The improved performance of Middle Eastern studies is something to be hoped for, even if America has come to look elsewhere for interpretations of the region. The field is still home to many talented, experienced, and knowledgeable people, who could contribute much more than they do, were they not burdened by dogma or pressured to conform. The field is ripe for change and awaits its reformers. If this critique makes their work easier, it will have served its purpose.

This first step could not have been taken by anyone teaching at an American university today. Middle Eastern studies used to resemble a quaint guild, emphasizing proficiency. Now they more closely resemble a popular front, demanding conformity. Professional success depends, in large part, upon deference to certain icons and their defense. And so this is unavoidably the work of an intimate stranger, one who, these last twenty-eight years, has entered and exited the American arena many times, first as a student, and later as an occasional visiting professor and research fellow. Its insights have been sharpened by the experience of directing a major (foreign) academic center for Middle Eastern studies, and observing the American campus many times from a Washington window.

Nearly thirty years ago, as a first-year undergraduate, I was assigned to read Elie Kedourie's essay, "The Chatham House Version." It was an exacting refutation of an entire school of error, one that rested on a nihilistic philosophy of Western guilt, articulated by a self-anointed priesthood of expertise. It captivated me then, as it does even now. In the years that followed, I witnessed my own chosen field fall under the spell of the same idea, propagated (as befits America) by celebrity professors and their fans. Since that time, "The best lack all conviction, while the worst / Are full of passionate intensity." But the spell is now diminished. Might it be broken?

Notes

1. Jerrold D. Green, "The Politics of Middle East Politics," *PS: Political Science* 27, no. 3 (September 1994), p. 517.

2. Jerrold D. Green, "Where Are the Arabs?" *Survival* 40, no. 2 (Summer 1998), p. 178.

3. James A. Bill, "The Study of Middle East Politics, 1946–1996: A Stocktaking," *Middle East Journal* 50, no. 4 (Autumn 1996), pp. 501, 507.

4. Lisa Anderson, "Politics in the Middle East: Opportunities and Limits in the Quest for Theory," in *Area Studies and Social Science: Strategies for Understanding Middle East Politics*, ed. Mark Tessler (Bloomington: Indiana University Press, 1999), p. 6.

5. Gary Sick, "The United States and Iran: Truth and Consequences," *Contention* 5, no. 2 (Winter 1996), p. 59.

6. In 1993, a foundation program officer wrote that the Israeli-Palestinian breakthrough would require Middle East specialists to "ask new questions, reexamine conventional wisdoms, explore new methods and approaches, and promote the development of research agendas capable of understanding and explaining the transformation represented by the [Israeli-Palestinian] agreement." See Steven Heydemann, "Peace and the Future of Middle East Studies," *Items* 47, no. 4 (December 1993), p. 78.

1

An American Invention

> This Committee, of course, looks forward to a time when the United States might lead the world in Near Eastern scholarship, when all the essential competences in the field—and they are very many—will be represented in American educational institutions, with adequate provision for their continuance and development, and with all the tools necessary to make them effective, not only in scientific, but in practical life.
> —*Committee on Near Eastern Studies (1949)*[1]

Fifty years ago, America invented Middle Eastern studies. The study of the lands that now constitute the Middle East had a long history in Europe, under the broad rubric of Oriental studies. It was a tradition with complex roots in the European experience of Crusade, Renaissance, and Enlightenment—the contexts for Europe's efforts to systematize the study of other peoples and places. In the first half of the twentieth century, an attempt was made to plant this rarified tradition in American soil, and it took root in a few isolated places. But Americans regarded this orientalism as formalistic and stuffy erudition and almost immediately set out to improve, adapt, streamline, modernize, and popularize it. The result became Middle Eastern studies—not only a variation on a theme, but its reinvention.

The present-day structure of Middle Eastern studies dates from the "bonanza years" of international and area studies, the 1950s and 1960s. Since that time, reputations have been made and lost, theories have been formed and abandoned, fads have come and gone, but the structure has remained the same. This structure probably constitutes the most unique contribution of American Middle Eastern studies. It certainly has been far more durable than the American-bred paradigms deployed to explain the Middle East itself. These have come and gone with an almost cyclical regularity, as if their obsolescence had been planned in advance. But the sturdy structure was built to last, and so it stands today, fundamentally unaltered. This was because the builders, whatever they understood or did not understand about the Middle East, did understand America. In particular, they understood what it took to get other Americans to support the systematic study of a distant part of the world, closer to the bottom of America's foreign priorities than to the top.

Formula for Success

Fifty years ago, Middle Eastern studies had not yet come into being. Here and there, on scattered American campuses, a handful of scholars dabbled in the modern Middle East. Ten years later, the academic landscape of America was dotted with Middle East centers and programs. Later myth held that "the foreign-policy community goaded or tempted the academic community into establishing graduate programs to generate useful expertise on such crucial foreign areas as the Middle East."[2] In the case of the Middle East, exactly the opposite was true: the academics did the goading and tempting.

This was because the Middle East did not figure very large in the post–Second World War policy concerns of the United States. In 1947, the Social Science Research Council (SSRC), the principal clearinghouse for applied social science, urged a "national program for area studies" covering the entire world. But "since we cannot at once develop first-class centers of study for every area, it would seem practical to attack the critical ones first." The "consensus of judgement" held these "critical areas for study" to be "the Far East, Russia, and Latin America."[3] In 1952, the political scientist Hans Morgenthau wrote that "practical needs" were "apparent in the selection of the areas most frequently studied. Russia and the Far East vie with Latin America for the attention of students and the commitment of resources." Initiatives for covering other areas came from "university administrations [that] have been known to search for empty spaces on the map which they might cover with an institute for area studies."[4]

In the late 1940s and early 1950s, the Middle East was precisely one such "empty space." In 1947, a dozen interested academics, alarmed at the prospect of being passed over, organized a Committee on Near Eastern Studies, under the auspices of the American Council of Learned Societies. "The judgments of American voters mean life or death for less powerful peoples in the Near East and elsewhere," they argued in their 1949 report. "No rational person would maintain that we should wield this decisive power blindly and ignorantly." The committee recommended "an immediate seven-point program for studies of the modern Near East," including fellowships, a language program, a translation program, and more.[5] The committee even inspired a *New York Times* article. There already existed centers for Chinese and Slavic studies, reported the *Times* correspondent. "Now an equally great demand has arisen for knowledge and information concerning the Near East."[6]

Yet despite the report, the "great demand" was not self-evident. In 1951, the chief of staff of the Senate Foreign Relations Committee gave a straightforward reply to one of the earliest appeals for government support of Middle Eastern studies. "If one looks over the legislative program since the war," he remarked, "he will find that Congress has had before it a good many important problems relating to various parts of the world, but very few relating to the Near East."[7] This attitude pervaded government, the universities, and the foundations. "In fact, we were always considered a 'minor' area," admitted one of the founders of the field, "something of a weak sister to the more obviously important Far Eastern and Eastern European areas."[8]

The challenge of the founders was to persuade the skeptical commanders of American wealth and power to invest in the study of what seemed like a remote and esoteric field. It was an uphill battle. But in the course of a decade, they succeeded in gaining the support of university administrations, private foundations, and, finally, the government. Academic entrepreneurship, not government initiative, launched Middle Eastern studies in America. Never were the leaders of Middle Eastern studies more inventive and responsive than in those early years, when support could not be taken for granted. Not since then have the leaders of Middle Eastern studies had so profound an understanding of what it takes to win a share of America's bounty.

They understood, first of all, that Americans divided the world into strategic areas, and that strategy played a more important role in American perceptions than either culture or religion. The term "Middle East" was itself the invention of an American naval strategist, who coined it in 1902. Governments eventually adopted the term. But until the middle of the century, the few academic departments that dealt with the region, most of them in old-line East Coast universities, described themselves as devoted to Oriental or Near Eastern studies.

While this evoked the learned traditions of Europe, it did little to excite the imagination of the American public. The Orient could be confused with the Far East, and the Near East evoked Assyrians and Nineveh no less than Arabs and the Persian Gulf. The founders understood that they needed a modern definition, for an America that divided the world into strategic areas. And so with few exceptions, the academic units created after the Second World War called themselves departments or centers for Middle Eastern studies. Under the guise of a twentieth-century American term, one could teach or research just about anything that transpired in the nearly fourteen centuries since the Prophet Muhammad. But the guise itself was an ingenious one, for it suggested that these studies were all somehow relevant to the needs of twentieth-century America.

Second, the founders understood the growing prestige that attached to the social sciences. Oriental studies had been a humanistic endeavor, and their claim to scientific stature rested rather narrowly on philological decipherment and the translation of texts. Americans generally viewed this kind of research as antiquarian, and it could never have generated much support for the field.

American Middle Eastern studies proposed to leave the demanding labor of philology and textual analysis to Europe. American academics would be *social* scientists; they would master the theories and paradigms of the new disciplines, supplemented by a working, practical knowledge of history and language. Scholars would plant at least one foot squarely in one of the prestigious new disciplines: political science, sociology, anthropology, and economics. Similarly, America's historians of the Middle East would differ from their European counterparts, in their explicit application of the exciting discoveries of the social sciences. And those still fascinated by languages would substitute linguistics for philology, employing the tools of the social sciences to establish the interaction of language and the contemporary scene. In that sense, they all would become more than scholars: they would become experts. Not only would this lend an additional aura of relevance to the fledgling field; it would secure a foothold for Middle Eastern studies in the disciplinary departments, the locus of academic appointments.

However, this was tempered by a third understanding: if something were worth doing in American academe, surely it had to have its own independent administration, funding, offices, secretaries, committees, and letterheads. Thus emerged the flagships of American Middle Eastern studies, the Middle East centers. The idea was simple: build a cross-disciplinary coalition of scholars interested in the Middle East, repackage them as a center under a distinguished "director," and go forth to raise funds. The centralized centers, headed by "directors," were another American invention, and a compelling alternative to the decentralized departments and their chairmen. Flexible programs also had more appeal to many donors than the fixed, endowed chairs of departments. The upstart centers raised many eyebrows in the established departments, and critics regarded them "as little more than skillfully constructed devices for collecting money."[9] But they did this extremely well, and they rapidly became most prominent features in the landscape of Middle Eastern studies.

Fourth, the founders had an appreciation for the vastness of America. Oriental studies in Europe had been geographically centered in or near the great capitals, in close proximity to various sources of patronage—royal, ecclesiastical, governmental, or commercial. But in America, sources of patronage were spread across the continent, in cities and states jealous of their civic standing. Even the national seat of power consisted of representatives from hundreds of constituencies coast to coast. Strength derived not from proximity to the capital, but from broad geographic dispersal.

And so the champions of Middle Eastern studies became enthusiastic homesteaders. The Middle East, they maintained, should be taught, researched, and understood not only on the eastern seaboard, but in Michigan, Illinois, Texas, and California. From there, academic homesteaders went forth to establish still more programs in Arizona, Utah, Oregon, and Washington state. Leaders of Middle Eastern studies knew how to play upon local pride, and skillfully persuaded university trustees that possession of one of their programs conferred prestige. And once these programs were spread across

America, these same leaders could pose as spokespersons of a nationwide network of activity, an advantage in dealings with New York foundations and Washington bureaucracies.

Fifth, the founders also understood the vital importance of coordinating this far-flung enterprise. In 1951, the Social Science Research Council founded the Committee for the Near and Middle East, and it undertook a host of activities for planning and coordination of the fledgling enterprise.[10] But this did not suffice to meet the needs of scattered scholars in dozens of institutions. Some sort of association would be needed, which would convene a national convention, elect officers, pass resolutions, and lobby legislators. In 1966, leaders of the field joined together to found the Middle East Studies Association of North America, known as MESA.

MESA's concept was purely American. In Europe, there had been "learned societies" that admitted scholars and antiquarians, and published "proceedings." In 1842, American enthusiasts of Oriental studies followed this model, establishing the American Oriental Society, the AOS. But the AOS gave priority to antiquity, and it lacked an enthusiasm for the social sciences. Nor did it have any provision for institutional membership. MESA welcomed just about everyone from any discipline and built a network of institutional affiliates. MESA published a journal, a bulletin, and a newsletter, and established a panoply of committees for research and training, ethics, and academic freedom. Its elected president and officers could purport to speak for Middle Eastern studies, and the MESA apparatus became something akin to a union for practitioners in the field.

Sixth, the founders understood the importance of leadership. The leaders of Middle Eastern studies, especially center directors, had to enjoy both academic credibility and public visibility. They had to be public figures, whose persona or work commanded respect beyond the campus. In any European country fifty years ago, only native-born scholars could claim such standing. Americans, in contrast, still stood in awe of the oracles of the Old World, who fell into two categories: the "wise men from the East," and the "great minds of Europe." The architects of Middle Eastern studies recruited both in their efforts to summon legitimacy, and did so with considerable success.

"Wise men" were scholars, usually from Arab lands, who had built careers on their claim to intimate and privileged insight into the strange ways of the (Middle) East. The pioneer was unquestionably Philip Hitti, a Lebanese-born historian. In 1944, Hitti became chair of Princeton's Department of Oriental Languages and Literatures, and in 1947, he established the Program in Near Eastern Studies, the country's first Middle East center. "There is hardly a center of Middle East studies in this country that has not followed the tradition of these studies which he established at Princeton University," related his obituary in the bulletin of MESA. "In a real sense he was the father of these studies in America."[11] Other Arab founders of Middle East centers included the Egyptian historian Aziz Atiya (University of Utah) and two jurists, the Iraqi Majid Khadduri (Johns Hopkins) and the Palestinian Farhat Ziadeh (University of Washington). These "wise men" were formidable leaders of Middle East centers, and their mastery of the finer points of culture and language commanded a special reverence, on campus and off.[12]

But association with one of the "great minds of Europe" could achieve the same effect. Worldly Europeans still radiated gravitas in America, and there was no surer way for a Middle East center to gain visibility than to bring a knight or an aristocrat across the Atlantic and place him at the head of the table. In 1955, Harvard imported the preeminent British orientalist Sir Hamilton A. R. Gibb to direct its new Center for Middle Eastern Studies. In 1957, UCLA hired the erudite Viennese cultural historian Gustave von Grunebaum to direct its new Center for Near Eastern Studies. (He had come to America twenty years earlier, in flight from the Nazis.) Transplanted "great minds" imparted old prestige to new enterprises that craved academic and public acceptance. Until about 1960, the "wise men" and the "great minds" fronted for the field as a whole. "For several decades," complained one political scientist in 1962, "we have been filling a portion of our needs by importing European and Middle Eastern scholars, who now compose an astonishingly high proportion of American faculties in this field."[13] The imported leaders brought stature and respectability. But as the field sought to affirm its relevance, the need arose for a leadership that enjoyed greater visibility in interpreting current events.

This goal was largely achieved by a third category, the "trained scientists." These were mostly social scientists, many of them American-born, who combined academic credentials with a specialization in the contemporary Middle East. The pioneer was the sociologist Morroe Berger, who directed Princeton's Program in Near Eastern Studies from 1962 and made it completely autonomous. At about that time, the political scientist Leonard Binder launched the University of Chicago's Committee on Middle Eastern Studies, precursor of its Center for Middle Eastern Studies. Others followed, and by the mid-1960s, with the establishment of MESA, the "trained scientists" assumed the role of leaders of the field. The transition created tensions, but it served the need of Middle Eastern studies to project themselves as relevant to wider concerns.

Seventh, and last, the founders knew how to frame their appeals in political terms that made sense to their fellow Americans. In the early years, this framework was the Cold War. Hitti at Princeton was an early expert at making Cold War appeals for academic institutions. In 1946, for example, he made a pitch for U.S. government support for American universities in the Middle East, with a warning against "the communist ideology which has been invading the Near East subtly and cleverly for several months—in fact, for several years." American universities, he announced, were "the most important vital force in the Near East at the present time for strengthening the liberal forces in their death struggle against the communist forces from outside and the feudal, sectarian forces from within." It was in "the interest of the government and the people of the United States to support to the limit" such "liberalizing agencies in the Near East."[14] In 1949, the Committee on Near Eastern Studies emphasized the location of the region, "just on the hither side of a civilization which is competing with our own for world leadership."[15] No one in the field recoiled from this kind of appeal because no other kind of appeal worked as well.

At the same time, at least some of the founders understood the danger to the enterprise of too overt an identification with Middle Eastern causes. Most of them had preferences, and a few had commitments. Hitti, for one, testified on the Palestine problem before Congress and the Anglo-American Commission of Inquiry and debated Albert Einstein over Palestine on the pages of the *Princeton Herald*.[16] But most scholars understood that overt partisanship would alienate university trustees, foundation heads, and government officials. In these early years, loyalty to the enterprise of Middle Eastern studies came first. The founders were usually careful to keep their own politics outside the fences they erected around the field. Middle Eastern studies, they were at pains to prove, did not serve Middle Eastern causes; they served the American cause in the Middle East, or simply served scholarship. In this effort, the founders enjoyed a modicum of success, and Middle Eastern studies did not gain their reputation for polarized partisanship until after the 1967 Arab-Israeli war, by which time the institutions of the field were fully established.

The Rewards of Relevance

The American formula for Middle Eastern studies constituted a brilliant invention. In a little more than a decade, Oriental studies had been revamped from top to bottom. The brand new network emphasized relevance; associated itself with the "scientific" disciplines; created high-profile centers of its own; spread its activities across the continent; created an association to link them all; mobilized imported dignitaries and academic entrepreneurs; and offered the entire package as a contribution to the national interest.

The innovative labors of the founders were amply rewarded. As the network took shape, America began to support it. The Carnegie and Rockefeller foundations liked what they saw, and opened their coffers to Middle Eastern studies (as they did to other area studies) from the late 1940s. From the 1950s, the Ford Foundation showered money on Middle East centers, graduate students, and later MESA.[17] From 1958, the federal government added more grants and fellowships, under Title VI of the National Defense Education Act (NDEA). And from 1962, the U.S. government allotted foreign currency surpluses to the massive acquisition of Arabic books, supplied for free to major research libraries.[18]

The results were astounding. In 1949, the Committee on Near Eastern Studies reported that "at no university does there appear to be a person who would claim to be an expert in the economics, sociology, or politics of the present-day Near East."[19] Twenty years later, in 1969, there were an estimated 340 full-time faculty members in Middle Eastern studies; in 1977, there were 530, a third of them in the "hard" social sciences.[20] In 1951, there were five Middle East programs at universities; in 1956, twelve; in 1962, eighteen; in 1970, thirty-six. In 1949, the Committee on Near Eastern Studies called for "university centers at which Near Eastern studies are more highly elaborated than elsewhere" and suggested that "three or four of these, properly spaced geographically, will suffice."[21] In 1959, Title VI supported three Middle East centers; in 1964, eight; in 1970, fifteen. Between 1959 and 1976, these centers produced 4,300 bachelor's degrees, 1,500 master's degrees, and 800 doctorates.[22] In the decade beginning in 1962, major research libraries tripled or quadrupled their Arabic holdings; the torrent of books overwhelmed some libraries, which reported difficulties in cataloguing them.

The scope of Princeton's program suggested how much money was involved. In the early 1960s, when it was directed by Morroe Berger (the first president of MESA), Princeton's Program in Near Eastern Studies received $120,000 a year from the Ford Foundation, $60,000 a year under Title VI, and $60,000 from corporations. (The Princeton program also drew upon a grant of half a million dollars made by the Rockefeller Foundation back in 1954.) These $240,000 would be the equivalent of $1.3 million today, for a unit with only fifteen faculty affiliates. With these funds, the Program supported nineteen students on external fellowships, convened an annual two-day conference, sponsored a book series at the university press, and much more.[23] Centers at Columbia, Harvard, Michigan, and UCLA achieved comparable levels of external funding.

So astonishing was the rapid American success that it reverberated even in Britain. In 1960, a delegation of Britain's Sub-Committee on Oriental, Slavonic, East European, and African Studies visited the United States. They had been charged with proposing the restructuring of area studies in Britain and wished to inspect how these studies had evolved on American shores. They visited ten American universities, including Harvard, Princeton, Columbia, Michigan, UCLA, and Berkeley, home to some of the country's leading Middle East centers. From their report, it was evident that American area studies—Middle Eastern studies not the least among them—had become the envy of the world.

Understated language could hardly conceal the enthusiasm of the visitors. They praised the leadership of the major foundations and stressed the commitment of the U.S. government. They were fascinated by the concept of area studies centers, and awed by the rapid expansion of fellowship programs, language institutes, and libraries. Ultimately, Britain would have no alternative but to emulate the superior American system, which gave "a practical demonstration of a different approach to the study of the non-Western world. The comparisons are provocative and prevent any complacency about developments here."[24] It was a testimony to the new preeminence of American area studies, and Middle Eastern studies were no exception.

By the time fifty-one founding fellows convened in New York in 1966 to establish MESA, they could look back upon twenty years of astonishing progress. In record time, they had built an academic empire, supported by the universities, the foundations, the corporations, and the taxpayers. They had persuaded influential constituencies that money spent on Middle Eastern studies was money well spent. And they had used these funds wisely, to found autonomous Middle East centers and programs. All that remained to be done was to fill this admirable vessel with content. It was at this point that Middle Eastern studies first ran into trouble.

The Dogma of Development

In 1964, J. C. Hurewitz, a political scientist at Columbia, described the accelerated effort to create Middle Eastern area studies in the fashionable jargon of the day. It "resembles a development program. In fact, it might amply be dubbed an American development program for our own underdeveloped studies of the underdeveloped areas of the world."[25]

For the founders, "development" (coupled with "modernization") was the privileged paradigm for understanding the Middle East. "All students of the Middle East turned into developers and modernizers," wrote one observer, "not to speak of redeemers and deliverers, of the Middle East."[26] Long before the contemporary Middle East became a subject of American study, it had been the subject of American missionary effort, accompanied by a belief in the bright prospects of political, social, and economic reform. Since the Middle East was bound to change, why not seek to influence the direction of change toward the values exemplified by America? These included liberal democracy, free markets, mild nationalism, and religious tolerance.

The paradigm of "development" served as the natural successor of the missionary tradition, and infused Middle Eastern studies with an American optimism. In the American tradition, this optimism was never naïve. It was calculated, self-interested, and "scientific." It also served a practical end in advancing the academic enterprise. A field with a message of can-do optimism was sure to command greater respect and resources from an America eager to see its ways emulated around the globe, especially in the cradles of Eastern civilization where the Soviet challenge loomed large.

So Middle Eastern studies were not only an academic field to be explored; they were also a message to be preached. The message varied in emphasis, and its theoretical ground often shifted, but it remained a fairly constant refrain: the feasibility and even inevitability of reform, development, and modernization. The set text of this approach was Daniel Lerner's *The Passing of Traditional Society* (1958), which argued that the Middle East had embarked on the linear path of the West: secularization, urbanization, industrialization, and popular participation. "What the West is," he wrote, "the Middle East seeks to become."[27] Malcolm Kerr later summarized "the liberal orientalists' conventional wisdom" as a belief that Muslims had "little choice but to learn from the West, to imitate, to borrow, to search out the secret of its progress, in order somehow to catch up."[28] And "the West" meant something very specific in the American context. "Theories [of modernization] describe what a modern society, polity, economy, and culture look like," wrote Leonard Binder, adding (in parentheses): "Generally, it looks like our country."[29]

"Modernization, it now appears, is harder than one supposed." Lerner made this admission six years after publication of his book. The problem, he concluded, was that people "don't do what, on any rational course of behavior, they should do."[30] In the Middle East, the driving forces of modernity were in clear evidence: accelerated urbanization, increased literacy, and exposure to the wider world through the mass media. But the responses defied ready explanation. Religious revivalists thwarted secularization, planners sacrificed industry to ideology, and regimes rejected any meaningful political participation. Time and again, the founders of Middle Eastern studies were embarrassed by the stubborn refusal of Middle Easterners, both rulers and ruled, to follow a "rational course." From an American perspective, the Middle East seemed to be moving sideways.

Lebanon delivered the first major blow to academic self-confidence. Lebanon, seat of the American University of Beirut (AUB), was that part of the Arab world the academics professed to know best, and they were certain it would achieve an American-like equilibrium. In 1963, Leonard Binder convened a major conference on "Lebanese Democracy" at the University of Chicago. Lebanon, he stressed, had "weathered the storm of ideological politics in the Arab world." Yet "few people credited Lebanese political achievements as the purposeful accomplishments of a mature political society."[31] As two anthropologists later wrote, American social scientists at the time "were entranced by Lebanon's apparent success in generating a free, capitalist, and pluralist society." Political scientists "waxed enthusiastic over the constitutional mediation of intergroup relations in Lebanon." To them, Lebanon looked like "ward politics writ large, tying together town and country, rich and poor, and guaranteeing admirable stability." American Middle East specialists of the 1950s and 1960s "completely overlooked or underestimated" the "seeds of civil conflict."[32] When Lebanon shattered in 1975, so did public confidence in its academic interpreters.

The debacle in Iran delivered a still more devastating blow. A few scholars were plainly pro-Pahlavi, and issued reassurances instead of warnings. Even as the revolution brewed, in 1978, the Hoover Institution at Stanford published a collected volume on Iran assembled by George Lenczowski, a political scientist at Berkeley and founder of its Middle East center. (A former Polish diplomat, he belonged to the category of imported "great minds.") In the book, a paean to Pahlavi rule, Lenczowski showered praise on Iran's "modernizing monarch." Thanks to Iran's reverence for monarchy, the country "possessed an advantage over some newer nations, which could not point to the same remarkable legacy. In the 1970s, half a century after the installation of the Pahlavi dynasty, this ancient legacy was being revived in its full dimensions."[33]

Nikki Keddie, historian of Iran at UCLA, has pointed out that such myopia was not limited to pro-regime scholars:

> U.S. scholars of modern Iran, who were doing research there in large numbers in the 1970s, did not predict anything like the revolution that occurred. This goes across the board for political scientists who interviewed both government and oppositional figures; economists who wrote of serious economic problems; and anthropologists, sociologists, and historians who looked at and listened to many classes of people, urban and rural, including clerics. These scholars, who were inclined to be critical of the shah's regime and not to echo official U.S. support for it, should, if anyone could, have provided predictions of serious trouble, but they did not.[34]

A revolution must defy prediction if it is to succeed, and the academics were hardly alone in failing to anticipate this one. But the Lebanese civil war and the Iranian revolution effectively decided the debate over the modernization and development theories which had been the stock-in-trade of American Middle Eastern studies: they had failed. Middle Eastern studies were left without a dominant paradigm, and vulnerable to academic insurgencies.

Yet the authors of this intellectual failure at least had institutional successes to their credit. One historian of the next generation put the ideas of his predecessors precisely in this context: "If the intellectually and theoretically insecure enterprise of Middle East Studies was to survive in the 1960s," he allowed, "a few bold, simple, and immediately useful ideas were needed to hold it together. That those ideas reflected American ideology and foreign policy concerns does them no discredit, for the academic enterprise was designed precisely to address such concerns. Unfortunately, both the enterprise and the ideas that undergird it fell short when it came to assessing the future."[35] The simple truth was that the academic empire of Middle Eastern studies could never have been built on anything but modernization and development theory, since no other paradigm enjoyed comparable stature in America during the 1950s and 1960s. Over the long term, it failed to explain or predict the Middle East. But over the short term, it filled the American landscape with Middle Eastern centers and programs that have survived to this very day.

Arabs and Israelis

Middle Eastern studies had more than paradigm troubles. From 1967, the Arab-Israeli conflict made for a deepening politicization of the field, clouding the reputation for disinterested objectivity so important to the founders. Arab politics before 1967 were, in the words of Malcolm Kerr, "like watching Princeton play Columbia in football on a muddy afternoon. The June war was like a disastrous game against Notre Dame which Princeton impulsively added to its schedule, leaving several players crippled for life." Henceforth, Arab politics "ceased to be fun."[36] Middle Eastern studies also lost much of their casual ambiance. The field had taken its first long strides during the Arab-Israeli standoff between 1949 and 1967. Most academics, like everyone else, had their preferences, but events did not compel professors to assert them. The 1967 war led many to do just that.

The new era was opened the following year, when George Hourani, a professor of philosophy and second president of MESA, delivered an openly political and polemical presidential address entitled "Palestine as a Problem of Ethics."[37] The following year, his successor, William Brinner, a Berkeley historian, used his presidential address to warn against a slide into politics: "We do not seek an end to controversy, but we must realize that the price we will pay for political involvement is the destruction of this young Association and the disappearance of a precious meeting place of ideas."[38] Later presidents showed more caution, but political partisanship remained an endemic problem in MESA, and every surge in the Arab-Israeli conflict inflamed political passions that surfaced in MESA's deliberations.[39]

That academics would differ over the conflict was unavoidable. But these differences were magnified and amplified by the emergence of Arab-Israeli relations as a prime field of teaching, research, and publication. A survey of a major index, including articles and books on the history of the Middle East published between 1962 and 1985, found that more than a third dealt with some aspect of the Arab-Israeli conflict.[40] The authors of these studies also preferred to teach the subject, and courses on the Arab-Israeli conflict (or, in later years, the Arab-Israeli peace process) proliferated on campuses.

An observer from abroad later described this as "the Arab-Israeli conflict/peace process industry of American academe."[41] Its post-1967 growth came at the expense of other countries and subjects, many of which suffered from relative neglect. But in the atmosphere of the 1970s, it became acceptable to teach one's political commitments, and courses on the Arab-Israeli conflict could always be justified by comparatively large enrollments. The fact that so much research and teaching revolved around the most divisive and emotive issue in the Middle East did little for the reputation of Middle Eastern studies in the disciplinary departments.

Nor did it help the field's broader reputation: by the 1970s, Arabs and Jews began to criticize academic programs and centers for allegedly substituting indoctrination for scholarship. Arabs complained that "the standard of objectivity in Middle East studies in the United States demands a decided bias in favor of Israel," and that "history and political science courses are numerically biased in favor of Israel and ignore large chunks of the Arab world."[42] Jews complained of "the omission of Israel or its minimalization" and "the general absence of courses on Israel or Zionism in the curricula of the Middle East centers."[43] Struggle over academic turf became a surrogate for war over Middle Eastern territory. Interested parties began to funnel money to academics, and watchdog groups subjected programs and centers to minute scrutiny, much to the consternation of deans and provosts.

"Someday peace may break out," warned Leonard Binder in his 1974 MESA presidential address, "and then people will cease to be willing to pay us to tell them what they want to hear. What will we then do if we have no scholarly standing?"[44] The problem was that peace tarried, crippling the development of Middle Eastern studies much as it crippled the development of the Middle East.

Debates and Standards

In addition to the political fallout from events in the Middle East, the founders faced serious problems at home. The growing autonomy of well-endowed centers alienated many of the humanists and orientalists in the teaching departments. At Princeton, for example, "the result was under-the-surface friction and competition between the two bodies that gave rise to gossip and backbiting," and that led several tenured faculty to leave the university.[45] In 1964, Columbia invited John Badeau, a former American ambassador to Egypt, to head its center, known as the Middle East Institute. "I did not know it at the time," Badeau later recalled, "but there had apparently been a good deal of friction between the Middle East Department and the Institute, and I was brought in the hope that some of this could be cured. . . . But nobody had ever told me about the situation and I was somewhat put out that I had not been warned."[46]

The social scientists who dominated the centers did not conceal their view that orientalism had been superseded. "Middle Eastern studies grew out of a tradition which, left unaltered, can only do harm," wrote the Princeton political scientist Manfred Halpern.[47] Chicago's Binder compared the attainments of the orientalists to "the monuments of the ancients which induce awe in us even though our technology far exceeds theirs."[48] But some orientalists were not at all certain they had been superseded by disciplinary "technology." In 1955, Wilfred Cantwell Smith, the Canadian Islamicist at McGill, expounded before the AOS on the "invalidity" of the disciplines, whose approach was marred by "preoccupation with the technique and methods rather than with the object of study, and, correspondingly, with manipulation and control rather than appreciation." The utilitarian bent of area studies had created a situation "full of danger, both to our studies and to the world. There is the danger of 'being used'; of subordinating knowledge to policy, rather than vice versa." And such knowledge, "pursued *ad majorem Americae gloriam* will, in the realm of oriental, as indeed in all human studies, fail to be sound knowledge."[49] MESA was formed in part because of the refusal of the AOS and orientalists like Smith to recognize Middle Eastern studies as their legitimate offspring.

This was compounded by the doubts within the disciplines about the validity of area studies. In the case of Middle Eastern studies, this manifested itself very concretely in the ambivalence demonstrated by Harvard, America's most prestigious university, to which others looked for leadership. When Gibb arrived in America in 1955, to direct Harvard's Center for Middle Eastern Studies, he had wanted to bring Oriental studies and the social sciences together. "But it was not long before I realised how inchoate, indeed how naïve, all my previous ideas had been, in face of the actual problems involved in developing a programme of area studies that could stand up to the high standards demanded by the Harvard Faculty—and equally so to the best academic standards in this country."[50] The departments were not willing to make permanent appointments in the field, and the center remained an improvisation, kept afloat by external funds. As one of Gibb's admirers put it, he was "not very successful" in integrating the center with the disciplinary departments, and so "his construction had the essential fragility of a network of patron-client relations."[51] A harsher judgement was that Gibb "failed in his mission at Harvard."[52] When Gibb departed in 1964, Harvard's center nearly folded, and for years it relied upon visiting faculty. Harvard tolerated its Middle East center (it brought in money), but never respected it.[53]

The failure of Middle Eastern studies to win full acceptance at the nation's most talked-about university constituted a major setback. Above all, it confirmed doubts elsewhere about the quality of practitioners who had been recruited in a rapid effort to build institutions from scratch. Academic empire-builders needed manpower to sustain the rapid expansion, and demand far exceeded supply. "To speak plainly," admitted Gibb, "there just are not yet enough fully-qualified specialists in any of the required fields to go round."[54] But appointments were made all the same, and it was not long before Middle Eastern studies earned a reputation for their toleration of low standards, a problem especially noticeable in the better universities.

The shortfall could not be quantified, but neither could it be denied. Leonard Binder, as head of MESA's Research and Training Committee in the mid-1970s, conveyed its essence: "Middle East studies seem to have more than their share of nonspecialized scholars and of nonscholarly specialists," he wrote.

> Part of the reason for this sorry state of affairs is the failure to apply firm academic standards during the recent period of rapidly induced growth of area specialists. Many accomplishments have occurred over the past 30 years of which we can be proud. But there are great extremes of achievement in this field, and it was awfully easy to become an area specialist and to get a job up until very recently.[55]

"It is painful for a Middle East specialist to admit the fact," wrote Bernard Lewis three years later, "but it is nevertheless inescapable. Professional advancement in Middle Eastern studies can be achieved with knowledge and skill well below what is normally required in other more developed fields or more frequented disciplines, where standards are established and maintained by a large number of competent professionals over long periods."[56] By the time Binder and Lewis formulated the problem, it was no longer news to university administrators and faculty.

The presence of so many tenured incompetents became a source of intergenerational resentment by the late 1960s: just when Middle East centers began to produce substantial numbers of better-trained graduates, universities retrenched and the job market went flat. The writing was already on the wall in 1970, when MESA's president urged his colleagues to "slow down the rush to create more centers and programs."[57] But graduate enrollments continued to expand, even as employment opportunities dwindled. At the end of the 1960s, two-thirds of new area studies Ph.D.s found academic positions. By the end of the 1970s, only half found academic slots. In 1979, a RAND report on the "marketplace" for area and language studies found a "national imbalance" between supply and demand, and recommended that "Ph.D.s who originally aimed for academic employment should give more consideration to prospects in other sectors of society."[58] In 1979, MESA proposed a jobs program to the federal government, asking that it subsidize short-term positions for new graduates at lesser schools.[59] Nothing came of the idea.

As the job struggle intensified, resentment began to spread among new graduates and graduate students. The crisis was most acute among those aspiring academics on the left who rejected the option of pursuing alternative careers in government or corporations. For them, there was no alternative but academe, and they were prepared to use every means to force open its doors. In 1971, stalwarts of the student left formed the Middle East Research and Information Project (MERIP), devoted to class analysis of Middle Eastern affairs. In 1975, it turned from the difficult objective of liberating the Middle East to the more practical agenda of liberating Middle Eastern studies. MERIP published a lengthy indictment entitled "Middle East Studies Network in the United States," setting off a tremor among students. "The Middle East studies network functions as an instrument of imperialism rather than as an objective discipline," the authors wrote. "It is an instrument of control over the peoples of the Middle East." The indictment named names, and denounced MESA's leading lights (above all, MESA president Binder) for practicing imperialist science.[60] A barely concealed current of academic grievance ran beneath this charge: students accused professors of oppressing the Middle East at just the moment when those professors could no longer guarantee them jobs.

External funding also plummeted. The Ford Foundation delivered the first blow in 1966, by terminating its International Research and Training Program. (In the peak years of the mid-1960s, the Ford Foundation spent four times as much as the government on area studies centers.) In the early 1970s, the government also cut funding drastically, although these funds were later restored. By 1977, external funding of area studies by the government and the Ford Foundation was only a fifth of what it had been (in constant dollars) a decade earlier.[61] Some leaders hesitated to admit that the reversal had occurred on their watch. "It is difficult to say whether we are facing a real crisis of funding," announced Binder in 1976.[62] But untenured faculty and graduate students had no difficulty in saying just that.

It was at this juncture that many centers and programs began to look to foreign governments for financial support. Iran and Arab Gulf countries had enjoyed a windfall after 1973, following the oil embargo and the spike in oil prices. But their image had been battered in America, where they were depicted as price-gouging extortionists. Leaders of Middle Eastern studies began to market their enterprise to these governments, suggesting that it might somehow improve the image of their foreign benefactors. For some of these governments, Middle Eastern studies were indeed an "instrument of control"—in this case, of American public opinion. The investments began to flow.

"It is unfortunately true," noted Binder in the mid-1970s, "that the wealthiest countries, with the exception of Iran, perhaps, are those that least value the Western ideal of scholarship."[63] Whether or not foreign governments learned the rules (and the shah's Iran had not mastered them either), their subsidies to Middle Eastern studies provoked controversies, which in turn drew the kind of press coverage every university dreads.[64] It was epitomized by a 1979 header in *Science*, the journal of the American Academy for the

Advancement of Science: "Oman, Qatar, and the United Arab Emirates are suddenly worth $tudying."[65] The captains of the field, desperate for new infusions of funds to keep their ships afloat, were reluctant to address the dilemma, and MESA remained silent as embarrassment followed embarrassment.

The fact that the most extreme example of such solicitation took place right in the nation's capital, at Georgetown University, further undermined the reputation of the field. Georgetown had missed the boom years of federal funding, and its small concentration of Middle East academics had no funded framework. Working hand in hand with a supportive administration, they decided to solicit every Arab government, without exception, for support for a new Center for Contemporary Arab Studies. The indiscriminate approach failed to make even the most fundamental distinctions among those governments. Gifts from Arab Gulf states created only minor ripples, but when a Georgetown mission successfully landed a major endowment from Libya in 1977, the rest of Washington was appalled. In 1981, a subsequent university administration returned the funds (with interest) to the Libyan government.[66] Georgetown's center was an agile adaptation of Middle Eastern studies in an era of retrenchment: in the absence of academic jobs, attract students by preparing them for professional careers; in the absence of American support, seek foreign funding. But the mistakes attending its creation did immense damage to the image of the field, persuading many Americans, on campus and off, that Middle Eastern studies were especially prone to a kind of intellectual corruption.[67]

A Vulnerable Enterprise

"This Committee, of course, looks forward to a time when the United States might lead the world in Near Eastern scholarship." A quarter of a century later, the dream of the Committee on Near Eastern Studies, expressed in 1949, seemed to have been fulfilled. Most Americans did not have to cross a state line to study Arabic or Persian, read the latest books from Cairo, or take degrees under distinguished foreign scholars or the Americans they had trained. For Europeans, and even Middle Easterners, America had become the mecca of Middle Eastern studies, a country that applied the best mix of talent, money, and freedom to the study of what had been an empty space on the American academic map.

But rapid growth, and the cycle of boom and bust, had exacted a price. Middle Eastern studies, which had supposedly come of age, labored under the weight of failed paradigms, creeping politicization, low standards, job scarcity, budget cutting, and borderline corruption. Binder put it bluntly to MESA's members in his 1974 presidential address: "The fact is that Middle Eastern studies are beset by subjective projections, displacements of affect, ideological distortion, romantic mystification, religious bias, as well as a great deal of incompetent scholarship."[68] Even a passing visitor could sense the doubts that afflicted the enterprise. A French scholar who visited America and prepared a survey of the field in 1978 found a "malaise amongst Middle East area specialists" in America. This malaise, catalyzed by the Arab-Israeli conflict and financial troubles, had "led certain establishments or departments to the verge of breakdown."[69]

"Malaise," of course, is the essential precondition for the advancement of scholarship. But did Middle Eastern studies have the intellectual wherewithal to reinvent themselves at the close of the 1970s? Earlier in the decade, the Research and Training Committee of MESA tried its hand at reconceptualizing the field and even establishing research priorities. It was a failed exercise: academics were prepared to join forces for institutional defense, but American academe had a strong aversion to the centralized "academy of sciences" approach to research priorities. Yet even without centralized prodding, there were signs that the "malaise" was beginning to generate alternative paradigms to "modernization," and alternative structures to the conventional Middle East center. Middle Eastern studies were in transition. Had they enjoyed the luxury of gradual evolution, they might well have created a new symbiosis, with greater power to explain the Middle East—after all, the ultimate purpose of the enterprise.

Instead, Middle Eastern studies came under a take-no-prisoners assault, which rejected the idea of objective standards, disguised the vice of politicization as the virtue of commitment, and replaced proficiency with ideology. The text that inspired the movement was entitled *Orientalism*, and the revolution it unleashed has crippled Middle Eastern studies to this day.

Notes

1. Committee on Near Eastern Studies, *A Program for Near Eastern Studies in the United States* (Washington, D.C.: American Council of Learned Societies, 1949), p. 33.

2. Richard W. Bulliet, book review in *Political Science Quarterly* 102, no. 1 (Spring 1987), p. 166.

3. Robert B. Hall, *Area Studies: With Special Reference to Their Implications for Research in the Social Sciences* (New York: Social Science Research Council, 1947), pp. 82–83.

4. Hans J. Morgenthau, "Area Studies and the Study of International Relations," *International Social Science Bulletin* 4, no. 4 (1952), pp. 647–48.

5. Committee on Near Eastern Studies, *A Program for Near Eastern Studies*, p. 6.

6. Benjamin Fine, "Council for Learned Societies Suggests a Plan for College Work on the Near East," *New York Times*, March 12, 1950.

7. Francis O. Wilcox, quoted by Mortimer Graves, "A Cultural Relations Policy in the Near East," in *The Near East and the Great Powers*, ed. Richard N. Frye (Cambridge: Harvard University Press, 1951), p. 79.

8. William M. Brinner, "1970 Presidential Address," *MESA Bulletin* 5, no. 1 (February 1, 1971), p. 3.

9. So these critics complained to a visiting delegation of Britain's University Grants Committee, *Report of the Sub-Committee on Oriental, Slavonic, East European, and African Studies* (London: Her Majesty's Stationery Office, 1961), p. 124.

10. The early years of the SSRC committee are described by J. C. Hurewitz, "The Education of J. C. Hurewitz," in *Paths to the Middle East: Ten Scholars Look Back*, ed. Thomas Naff (Albany: State University of New York Press, 1993), pp. 96–103.

11. Farhat J. Ziadeh, "Philip Khuri Hitti," *MESA Bulletin* 13, no. 1 (July 1979), pp. 1–2.

12. Later, it would be important to younger Arab-American academics, eager to claim exclusion, to denigrate the contribution made by these scholars. The Association of Arab-American University Graduates, in launching its own journal in 1979, dismissed those who had gone before:

    > Insofar as there is now a sizeable population of Arabs resident in the West, then this population has hitherto played the subordinate role of native informants to the dominant corps of Western experts. In this secondary position, for one reason or another Arabs have been cooperative. Perhaps they have felt so estranged and so ill at ease in a society given as by definition superior to theirs that all they could do was to follow along in docility and humble discipleship.

    The Editors, "Why ASQ?" *Arab Studies Quarterly* 1, no. 1 (Winter 1979), p. iv. This condescending caricature of an earlier generation suggested that Arab-Americans had been victims of a systematic discrimination and were thus entitled to redress. In fact, it did an immense injustice to those Arab-Americans—neither docile nor humble—who had pioneered the field as founders and leaders.

13. Manfred Halpern, "Middle Eastern Studies: A Review of the State of the Field with a Few Examples," *World Politics* 15, no. 1 (October 1962), p. 119.

14. "Remarks by Dr. Philip K. Hitti on His Near Eastern Mission," *Near East Colleges Quarterly* 10 (October 1946), p. 7.

15. Committee on Near Eastern Studies, *A Program for Near Eastern Studies*, p. 6.

16. R. Bayly Winder, "Philip Khuri Hitti (1886–1978): An Homage," in *Crossing the Waters: Arabic-Speaking Immigrants to the United States before 1940*, ed. Eric J. Hoogland (Washington, D.C.: Smithsonian Institution Press, 1987), p. 152. Hitti's papers are archived at the Immigration History Research Center at the University of Minnesota.

17. David R. Smock, "Ford Foundation Support for Middle Eastern Studies in the U.S.," *MESA Bulletin* 10, no. 1 (February 1, 1976), pp. 20–25. Ford's fellowship grants were administered through the SSRC. Ford's institution-building grants went to Middle East centers at Berkeley, Chicago, Columbia, Harvard, Michigan, New York University, Pennsylvania, Princeton, and UCLA.

18. David H. Partington, "Arabic Library Collections: A Study of the P.L. 480 Program," *MESA Bulletin* 9, no. 1 (February 1, 1975), pp. 12–29.

19. Committee on Near Eastern Studies, *A Program for Near Eastern Studies*, p. 8.

20. This is R. Bayly Winder's estimate in "Four Decades of Middle Eastern Study," *Middle East Journal* 41, no. 1 (Winter 1987), p. 47. His figure was extrapolated from MESA's rolls.

21. Committee on Near Eastern Studies, *A Program for Near Eastern Studies*, pp. 34–35.

22. Comptroller General, *Study of Foreign Languages and Related Areas: Federal Support, Administration, Need* (Washington, D.C.: U.S. General Accounting Office, September 1978), p. 21 (table 4).

23. Figures compiled by Larry Moses, *Language and Area Study Programs in American Universities* (Washington, D.C.: Department of State, 1964), p. 96.

24. University Grants Committee, *Report of the Sub-Committee*, p. 53. This became known as the Hayter Report, after the chairman of the committee, Sir William Hayter.

25. J. C. Hurewitz, "Undergraduate Foreign Area Studies: The Case of the Middle East— Report on a Conference," *American Council of Learned Societies Newsletter* 15, no. 4 (April 1964), p. 4.

26. P. J. Vatikiotis, "Middle Eastern Studies in America: A Memorandum," *Washington Review* 1, no. 1 (January 1978), p. 92.

27. Daniel Lerner, *The Passing of Traditional Society: Modernizing the Middle East* (New York: Free Press, 1958), p. 47.

28. Malcolm H. Kerr, "Arab Society and the West," in *The Shaping of an Arab Statesman: Abd al-Hamid Sharaf and the Modern Arab World*, ed. Patrick Seale (London: Quartet Books, 1983), p. 214.

29. Leonard Binder, "The Theory of Political Development," in *The Social Sciences and Problems of Development*, ed. Khodadad Farmanfamaian (Princeton: Princeton University Program in Near Eastern Studies, 1976), p. 72.

30. In the preface to the 1964 paperback edition, p. vii.

31. Leonard Binder, "Preface," in *Politics in Lebanon*, ed. Leonard Binder (New York: John Wiley, 1966), p. vii.

32. Elizabeth Warnock Fernea and Robert A. Fernea, *The Arab World: Personal Encounters* (Garden City, N.Y.: Anchor, 1987), pp. 31–32. This was a blindness to which specialists alone seemed vulnerable. The most prophetic insight into Lebanese politics in the Binder volume came from the one nonspecialist, University of Chicago political scientist Edward Shils, who dared to point out "the deficient civility of Lebanese society. Lebanon is not a civil society" because Lebanese accorded primacy to "communities of belief and primordial attachment." As a result, wrote Shils, Lebanese society "revolves round an empty center," and the country had to "be kept completely still politically" in order to prevent distrust from exploding. Edward Shils, "The Prospect for Lebanese Civility," in *Politics in Lebanon*, pp. 2, 4.

33. George Lenczowski, "Political Process and Institutions in Iran: The Second Pahlavi Kingship," in *Iran Under the Pahlavis*, ed. George Lenczowski (Stanford: Hoover Institution Press, 1978), p. 475.

34. Nikki R. Keddie, *Iran and the Muslim World: Resistance and Revolution* (New York: New York University Press, 1995), p. 13.

35. Richard W. Bulliet, "Twenty Years of Islamic Politics," *Middle East Journal* 53, no. 2 (Spring 1999), p. 191.

36. Malcolm Kerr, *The Arab Cold War: Gamal 'Abd al-Nasir and His Rivals, 1958–1970*, 3d ed. (London: Oxford University Press, 1971), p. v.

37. George F. Hourani, "Palestine as a Problem of Ethics," *MESA Bulletin* 3, no. 1 (February 15, 1969), pp. 15–25.

38. Brinner, "1970 Presidential Address," p. 7.

39. For example, upon eruption of the Palestinian *intifada* in 1987, some members felt strongly that MESA should pass resolutions; MESA's president, William B. Quandt— himself an authority on the Palestinians—felt compelled to warn that "we should not

allow MESA to become politicized in this way." William B. Quandt, "President's Column," *MESA Newsletter* 10, no. 2 (Spring 1988), p. 1.

40. Kenneth W. Stein, "The Study of Middle Eastern History in the United States," *Jerusalem Quarterly* 46 (Spring 1988), p. 61. The index was *Historical Abstracts*.

41. Eugene Rogan, "No Debate: Middle East Studies in Europe," *Middle East Report* 27, no. 4 (October–December 1997), p. 23.

42. Tareq Y. Ismael and Jacqueline S. Ismael, "Middle Eastern Studies in the United States," in *Middle East Studies: International Perspectives on the State of the Art*, ed. Tareq Y. Ismael (New York: Praeger, 1990), pp. 14, 17.

43. Academy for Educational Development, "Middle East Centers at Selected American Universities: A Report Presented by the American Jewish Committee" (unpublished report, July 1981), pp. 38–39.

44. Leonard Binder, "1974 Presidential Address," *MESA Bulletin* 9, no. 1 (February 1, 1975), p. 11.

45. Farhat Ziadeh, "Winds Blow Where Ships Do Not Wish to Go," in *Paths to the Middle East*, p. 315.

46. John S. Badeau, *The Middle East Remembered* (Washington, D.C.: The Middle East Institute, 1983), p. 251.

47. Halpern, "Middle Eastern Studies," p. 121.

48. Binder, "1974 Presidential Address," p. 2; idem, "Area Studies: A Critical Reassessment," in *The Study of the Middle East: Research and Scholarship in the Humanities and Social Sciences*, ed. Leonard Binder (New York: Wiley, 1976), p. 9.

49. Wilfred Cantwell Smith, "The Place of Oriental Studies in a Western University," *Diogenes* 16 (1956), p. 108.

50. Sir Hamilton Gibb, *Area Studies Reconsidered* (London: School of Oriental and African Studies, 1963), p. 4.

51. Albert Hourani, "H. A. R. Gibb: The Vocation of an Orientalist," in *Europe and the Middle East*, ed. Albert Hourani (Berkeley: University of California Press, 1980), pp. 130–31.

52. Vatikiotis, "Middle Eastern Studies in America," p. 90.

53. The Center's post-Gibb tribulations were the subject of an anonymous exposé, "Commander of the Faithful at Harvard," *New Middle East* 5 (February 1969), pp. 49–51.

54. Gibb, *Area Studies Reconsidered*, p. 16.

55. Binder, "Area Studies," pp. 6–7.

56. Bernard Lewis, "The State of Middle Eastern Studies," *American Scholar* 48, no. 3 (Summer 1979), pp. 372–73.

57. Brinner, "1970 Presidential Address," p. 4.

58. Sue E. Berryman, Paul E. Langer, John Pincus, and Richard H. Solomon, *Foreign Language and International Studies Specialists: The Marketplace and National Policy* (Santa Monica: RAND, September 1979), p. 63.

59. "Statement of MESA on the Future of Federal Support for Foreign Area Studies," *MESA Bulletin* 13, no. 2 (December 1979), pp. 111–12.

60. [Peter Johnson and Judith Tucker], "Middle East Studies Network in the United States," *MERIP Reports* 38 (1975), p. 20.

61. Berryman et al., *Foreign Language and International Studies Specialists*, p. viii ("external support is now stabilized in constant dollars at perhaps 20 percent of the peak levels of 1967"). See also fig. 2.2 on p. 43, mapping the near collapse of external support.

62. Binder, "Area Studies," p. 3.

63. Ibid.

64. See, for example, Larry Van Dyne, "U.S. Universities Try Mideast Grantsmanship," *Chronicle of Higher Education*, May 17, 1976; Gene I. Maeroff, "Mideast Gifts to U.S. Schools Pose Questions of Influence," *New York Times*, May 23, 1978; Seth Cropsey, "Arab Money and the Universities," *Commentary* (April 1979), pp. 72–74; Linda McQuaig, "A Tempting Knock at the Campus Gates," *Maclean's*, March 29, 1982; Fredelle Z. Spiegel, "Arab Influence on Middle East Studies in the U.S.," *Jerusalem Quarterly* 32 (Summer 1984), pp. 48–65.

65. R. Jeffrey Smith, "Middle East Investments in American Universities Spark Campus Confrontations," *Science* 203 (February 2, 1979), p. 421.

66. Gene I. Maeroff, "University Returns $600,000 Libyan Gift," *New York Times*, February 24, 1981.

67. For the "miserable public relations failure" at Georgetown, see Nicholas Lemann, "War-Torn Georgetown," *New Republic*, June 2, 1979, pp. 16–19. Georgetown's Center reminded Lemann of "a fairly sophisticated and professional think-tank with a political point of view, sort of an American Enterprise Institute for the Arab cause." Given the contemporary emphasis of the Center, he thought its support by Arab governments was "roughly equivalent to John D. Rockefeller financing a center in 1900 devoted to the study of Standard Oil and the antitrust question." When Arab money got tight in the 1990s, Georgetown's Center repackaged itself as a kind of general Middle East center in the hope of qualifying for federal support. In 1997, in the ultimate irony, it finally succeeded in becoming the "core" of a federally funded Title VI Middle East center.

68. Binder, "1974 Presidential Address," p. 8.

69. Irène Errera-Hoechstetter, "Middle Eastern Studies in the United States: One Country's Experience," *Journal of Area Studies* 2 (Autumn 1980), p. 18.

2

Said's Splash

This book reminds me of the television program *Athletes in Action*, in which professional football players compete in swimming, and so forth. Edward Said, a literary critic loaded with talent, has certainly made a splash, but with this sort of effort he's not going to win any races.
—*Malcolm Kerr on* Orientalism *(1980)*[1]

In 1978, Edward Said, a professor of English and comparative literature at Columbia University, published a book entitled *Orientalism*. Said did not emerge from the ranks of Middle Eastern studies. He was born in British-mandated Palestine, but spent most of his childhood in Egypt in thoroughly Anglophone surroundings. He then went to America for preparatory school, took his undergraduate degree at Princeton, finished his graduate studies at Harvard, and began to teach at Columbia. Said first made his academic way within the narrow confines of literary theory. "Until the June 1967 war I was completely caught up in the life of a young professor of English," wrote Said. But "beginning in 1968, I started to think, write, and travel as someone who felt himself to be directly involved in the renaissance of Palestinian life and politics."[2] So began a process of self-reinvention, as Said set out to establish his Palestinian identity.

Said visited Amman in the summers of 1969 and 1970, a heady time when Palestinian groups sought to turn Jordan into an armed base. They would be the force for change throughout the Middle East—so Said then believed and wrote—and the political cause of Palestine gradually claimed more of his prodigious output. After 1970, the retrenchment of the Palestinian resistance in Lebanon put it cheek-to-jowl with the long-standing American presence in that country. As the 1970s unfolded, Beirut loomed larger in Said's travels, and he spent a sabbatical year there in 1972–73. It was there that he began to learn literary Arabic in a systematic way.

In the years that followed, Said evolved into a public intellectual, meeting the growing American demand for a Palestinian perspective. Liberal opinion inside the media began to divide over Israel's policies after 1967, but split following the election of a rightist Israeli government in 1977. Publishers, journalists, and newscasters began to seek out articulate (and, preferably, angry) Palestinian voices. Said, positioned within taxi distance of the media's Manhattan epicenter, seized the opportunity. He would later complain that Palestinians were systematically denied "permission to narrate" their own story. But once Said made Palestine his part-time career, the media gave him no permission to rest. As one of his own disciples complained (in a tribute to Said), "when the question of Palestine is concerned, there is almost no limit to the intrusiveness and persistence of television and radio producers, journalists, and interviewers."[3] Said was combative in argumentation and concise in formulation, and he entered their Rolodexes immediately.

The Orientalism Debate

Had Said kept his political and professional commitments separate, he would have remained one more advocate of Palestine in the West—articulate in a way most likely to appeal to intellectuals, contentious in a way most appropriate to the political weeklies, op-ed pages, and *Nightline*, yet still a specimen of American ethnic politics.

But in his *Orientalism*, Said blended Palestinian passion and academic virtuosity so that they reinforced one another. The appeal of *Orientalism* resided, in part, upon its combination of political polemic and literary excursion. Said hailed from some point in the East ("this study derives from my awareness of being an 'Oriental'"), but he was also the Parr Professor of English and Comparative Literature, who announced in his introduction to *Orientalism* that he wrote it in his double capacity.[4] It was this quality which assured that this book, unlike his previous work, would be read across disciplinary boundaries and even by a general public.

In *Orientalism*, Said situated the Palestinians in a much wider context. They were but the latest victims of a deep-seated prejudice against the Arabs, Islam, and the East more generally—a prejudice so systematic and coherent that it deserved to be described as "Orientalism," the intellectual and moral equivalent of anti-Semitism. Until Said, orientalism was generally understood to refer to academic Oriental studies in the older, European tradition. (For art historians and collectors, it referred to paintings of Oriental themes, a facet of nineteenth-century romanticism.) Said resurrected and resemanticized the term, defining it as a supremacist ideology of difference, articulated in the West to justify its dominion over the East. Orientalism, according to Said, was racism of a deceptively subtle kind, and he sought to demonstrate its pervasiveness and continuity "since the time of Homer," but especially from the Enlightenment to the present. For most of this period, announced Said, "every European, in what he could say about the Orient, was a racist, an imperialist, and almost totally ethnocentric."[5]

To argue his point, Said amassed widely diverse examples from literature and scholarship, in a pyrotechnic display of erudition that refused all discrimination among genres and disregarded all extant hierarchies of knowledge. As one critic put it: "Who, after all, had ever thought that Lamartine and Olivia Manning, Chateaubriand and Byron, Carlyle, Camus, Voltaire, Gertrude Bell, the anonymous composers of *El Cid* and the *Chanson de Roland*, Arabists like Gibb, colonial rulers such as Cromer and Balfour, sundry quasi-literary figures like Edward Lane, scholars of Sufism like Massignon, Henry Kissinger—all belonged in the same archive and composed a deeply unified discursive formation!"[6] In Said's account, their texts interacted, and none of them was free of the hostile prejudgment of the Orient pervasive throughout Western culture.

Most important of all, Said included scholarly orientalism in his scope, and even accorded it a crucial role in disseminating orientalist dogmas. This scholarship, claimed Said, validated and fed the popular orientalism of the poets, novelists, travellers, and painters. The self-image of the scholars as truth-seeking investigators was a fraudulent façade, behind which lurked a sordid tale of complicity with power and acquiescence in the idea of Western supremacy. Scholars willingly or inadvertently collaborated with European governments in the promotion and justification of empire-building in Arab and Muslim lands. None of them, even the most accomplished and well intentioned, could escape the corrupting effects of power upon knowledge. While other sciences advanced, scholarly orientalism remained an instance of arrested development, itself the consequence of a view of Arabs and Muslims as arrested in their development. "Knowledge of the academic variety does not progress," concluded Said in 1981. "I think we should open knowledge to the non-expert."[7]

Over the last twenty years, Said's notion of a unified discourse of orientalism has been subjected to systematic criticism on numerous counts, and from many disciplinary vantage points.[8] Most criticisms come together on one point: Said selected only the evidence he needed to establish the existence of the "discursive formation" he named "Orientalism." He ignored the mass of evidence, including texts crucial to any history of literature or scholarship, that stood in the way of his polemical thrust. This evidence would have toppled Said's thesis, since it demonstrated that the Western understanding and representation of the East—especially the Arabs and Islam—had grown ever more ambivalent, nuanced, and diverse. Orientalism did not exhaust modern European ideas about Muslims and Arabs, any more than anti-Semitism exhausted modern Europe's ideas about Jews. Nor did the West "gaze" upon the East in a closed circle of interpretation. Time and again, new ideas generated by contact across cultures destabilized *a priori* assumptions. While prejudices and stereotypes were endemic, they never congealed into an unchanging, unified discourse on the Orient, even less a coherent "ideology of difference." And scholars, in particular, often took the lead in undermining anti-Oriental prejudices.

Bernard Lewis, Maxime Rodinson, Jacques Berque, W. Montgomery Watt, and Albert Hourani—doyens of Middle Eastern and Islamic studies in the European tradition—reached a similar conclusion about *Orientalism* from very different points of departure. Each of them regarded Said's treatment as a deeply flawed account of Western scholarship on the Arab and Islamic East, and some of them wrote alternative interpretations. Lewis, whom Said attacked in *Orientalism*, wrote a fighting reply, intended to demonstrate that Said had utterly distorted the history of scholarship. "The tragedy of Mr. Said's *Orientalism*," concluded Lewis, "is that it takes a genuine problem of real importance and reduces it to the level of political polemic and personal abuse."[9] The French historian Rodinson, whom Said praised in *Orientalism* (and later in *Covering Islam)*, wrote that "as usual, [Said's] militant stand leads him repeatedly to make excessive statements"—a failing exacerbated by the fact that Said was "inadequately versed in the practical work of the Orientalists."[10] The French scholar Jacques Berque, also praised in *Orientalism*, announced that Said had "done quite a disservice to his countrymen in allowing them to believe in a Western intelligence coalition against them."[11] The British Islamicist Watt (not mentioned in *Orientalism*) found Said guilty of "dubious or erroneous ascription of motives to writers," and felt compelled to point out "Said's ignorance of Islam."[12]

Most tellingly, the British historian Hourani—a man for whom Said expressed an abiding respect in *Orientalism* and elsewhere—also had serious misgivings about the book. He regretted its title: "Orientalism has now become a dirty word. Nevertheless it should be used for a perfectly respected discipline." He regretted the book's extremism: "I think [Said] carries it too far when he says that the orientalists delivered the Orient bound to the imperial powers." And he regretted the book's omissions: "Edward totally ignores the German tradition and philosophy of history which was the central tradition of the orientalists." One did not have to read too much between the lines to decipher Hourani's final verdict on *Orientalism*: "I think Edward's other books are admirable. The one on the question of Palestine is very good indeed because there he is on firm ground."[13]

Across the board, the most incisive criticisms of *Orientalism* originated in Europe, where many readers stood on firm (and familiar) ground. But in America, *Orientalism* became a best-seller, the canonical text of a field known as postcolonial studies. It inspired countless books, theses, and undergraduate papers; it was endlessly cited, quoted, and acknowledged. (The American historian David Gordon aptly described *Orientalism* as "a work that in certain circles has been almost Koranic in its prestige.")[14] *Orientalism* was a phenomenon, and it gradually insinuated its way to the top of the class in Middle Eastern studies. "1978 was a very good year for landmark books on the Middle East," announced Philip Khoury, then president of MESA, in his 1998 presidential address. "Edward Said's *Orientalism* also appeared that year. I wonder if there's been a better year since?"[15] The story of the career of *Orientalism*—how and why it *did* win the race—is the story of how the founders of Middle Eastern studies in America lost their composure. It is also, above all, an American tale.

Only in America

A British historian of India, Clive Dewey, looking back with twenty years of hindsight, wrote this of *Orientalism*:

> When Edward Said's *Orientalism* first appeared in 1978, historian after historian must have put it down without finishing it—without imagining, for a moment, the influence it would exert. It was, technically, so bad; in every respect, in its use of sources, in its deductions, it lacked rigour and balance. The outcome was a caricature of Western knowledge of the Orient, driven by an overtly political agenda. Yet it clearly touched a deep vein of vulgar prejudice running through American academe.[16]

Despite the fact that the bulk of *Orientalism* dealt with a chapter in the intellectual history of Europe, the book had its most profound and lasting impact in America. The "vulgar prejudice" to which Dewey alluded arose from the bitter struggle for academic hegemony in the humanities and social sciences on American campuses. As the students of the 1960s became the junior faculty of the 1970s, the academic center moved leftward. Academization translated radical political agendas into the theoretical framework of postmodernism, which postulated the subjectivity and relativity of all knowledge. In a time of diminishing opportunities in academe, this challenge increasingly took the form of an insurgency, which ultimately overran university departments in the humanities and social sciences.

Said's *Orientalism*, far from bucking convention, actually rode the crest of this immensely successful academic uprising. "I have found it useful here to employ Michel Foucault's notion of a discourse, as described by him in *The Archaeology of Knowledge* and in *Discipline and Punish*, to identify Orientalism."[17] Said's reverential nod to the French philosopher Foucault in his introduction followed an endorsement on the jacket of *Orientalism*, which declared it "the only American book thus far which can be compared to [Foucault's] powerful 'archaeologies' of social and intellectual exclusion."[18] In the 1970s, Foucault's major works began to appear in translation in American editions (from Pantheon, publisher of *Orientalism*), and the markers strategically placed around *Orientalism* were intended to associate the book with a set of concepts then sweeping through large parts of American academe. "I do not understand why [Said's] book had such success in the United States," wondered Rodinson in Paris. "The average American is not interested in orientalism."[19] But a growing number of average American academics had just read or heard of Foucault for the first time, and were drawn to this first American extrapolation—despite what the jacket endorsement frankly called "the limits of this particular subject matter."

Said partly overcame the limits of the subject matter by managing to quote, at least once, many of the English and French authors whose works are the staples of introductory literature courses. Yes, he would deal with orientalist scholars whose names meant nothing to American instructors and students. But readers would be enticed to turn the page by the expectation of a sudden encounter with Chateaubriand, Nerval, or Flaubert. This meant that *Orientalism* could be integrated easily into introductory curricula in English and French literatures, especially in their less demanding American varieties.

Orientalism also arrived at a crucial moment in the evolution of third worldism in American academe. By 1978, the enthusiasm for third world revolutions had ebbed among American intellectuals. (It would decline still further in the 1980s, when the third world produced a retrograde revolution in Iran and an anti-Soviet insurgency in Afghanistan.) But an entire generation of leftist scholars nurtured on radical commitments had already made their way through doctoral programs, and desperately needed a manifesto to carry them over the next hurdle.

Said was perfectly positioned to legitimize at least some of the contentions of the "critical scholarship" of the left. For while Said cultivated his image as an outsider ("To the West, which is where I live, to be a Palestinian is in political terms to be an outlaw of sorts, or at any rate an outsider"),[20] he was in fact the quintessential institutional insider: a chaired professor, in a leading department, at a prestigious university, in the greatest metropolis. *Orientalism* had the authority of "one of the country's most distinguished literary critics" (the book jacket), and while Said did not explicitly sanction all of the "critical scholarship," he did make deans and publishers wonder whether they could afford to do without one of its practitioners. For these younger academics, battling for university appointments, the publication of *Orientalism* was nothing less than "a seminal event, causing lasting reverberations throughout the academy."[21]

Orientalism also delegitimized the genealogy of established scholarship—and its current practitioners. This certainly was part of the appeal of the book, which in its last chapter, entitled "Orientalism Now," unsealed all its indictments. Said was a Palestinian intellectual (by choice), but he was also a New York intellectual (by habit). He understood—far better than many of his targets—that understatement went only so far in American academe. Allusions are most effective in smaller academic settings, where an efficient oral network of rumor and innuendo allows readers to fill in names by themselves. But Said understood that in the vastness of America, the published text should leave nothing to the imagination. And so *Orientalism* named names. Many readers must have gone straight to the index in search of themselves, their colleagues, or their teachers.

The delegitimation unfolded in a striking passage that effectively cancelled the validity of any Western scholarship on the East: "For a European or American studying the Orient there can be no disclaiming the main circumstances of *his* actuality: that he comes up against the Orient as a European or American first, as an individual second."[22] Any literary artifact, artistic creation, or academic product generated by a European or American continued to be "somehow tinged and impressed with, violated by, the gross political fact" of Western domination over the East.[23] There were no exceptions: wherever orientalism was not "manifest," Said determined that it was "latent." He thus saw no need to delve deeply into the complicated history of Western scholarship (this would not suit "my descriptive and political interests").[24] Instead, Said skimmed across its surface in search of the most offensive quotes, presented as the core or essence of orientalism, whose gravitational field no Westerner could hope to escape.

This argument also had practical implications. *Orientalism* appeared at a time when new minorities were seeking equitable if not preferential access to academe. Among them were Arabs and Muslims, for whom the field of Arab and Islamic studies had always been an obvious avenue for entry into the university. *Orientalism* gave them a step up. For who could escape the bind of orientalism, if not its ostensible victims, the Orientals themselves? A South Asian critic of *Orientalism*, Aijaz Ahmad, explained the book's operative importance within the university in this way:

> Its most passionate following in the metropolitan countries is within those sectors of the university intelligentsia which either originate in the ethnic minorities or affiliate themselves ideologically with the academic sections of those minorities. . . . These [immigrants] who came as graduate students and then joined the faculties, especially in the Humanities and Social Sciences, tended to come from upper classes in their home countries. In the process of relocating themselves in the metropolitan countries they needed documents of their assertion, proof that they had always been oppressed. . . . What the upwardly mobile professionals in this new immigration needed were narratives of oppression that would get them preferential treatment, reserved jobs, higher salaries in the social position they already occupied: namely, as middle-class professionals, mostly male. For such purposes, *Orientalism* was the perfect narrative.[25]

Middle Easterners, and especially Arab-Americans, had been in the first rank of the founders of Middle Eastern studies in America, and had long entered the university precisely through the Arab and Islamic field. (A recent president of MESA summarized his experience this way: "I cannot claim any discrimination against me in my youth [or for that matter as an adult] owing to my being an Arab-American.")[26] But they had not enjoyed *automatic* preference over others. *Orientalism* implicitly claimed for them a privileged understanding of the Arab and Islamic East, due not to any individual competence, but to their collective innocence of orientalist bias. They were unspoiled; they were entitled.

Knowledge and Power

From the general, Said proceeded to the specific: the development of Middle Eastern studies in America. *Orientalism* made two claims. First, Said determined that American Middle Eastern studies "retains, in most of its general as well as its detailed functioning, the traditional orientalist outlook which had been developed in Europe"—the outlook he had presented (or caricatured) in his book. "The European tradition of Orientalist scholarship was, if not taken over, then accommodated, normalized, domesticated, and popularized and fed into the postwar efflorescence of Near Eastern studies in the United States."[27] In the oceanic crossing, this tradition traded its old philological cloak for the fashionable garb of the social sciences. ("Enter the social scientist and the new expert," wrote Said, "on whose somewhat narrower shoulders was to fall the mantle of Orientalism.")[28] But "the core of the Orientalist dogma" remained intact.[29] This meant that Middle Eastern studies in America suffered from the same genetic defect as its European parent.

Second, Said represented Middle Eastern studies in America as a tightly integrated "establishment," which maintained dominance through invisible networks:

> There is of course a Middle East studies establishment, a pool of interests, "old boy" or "expert" networks linking corporate business, the foundations, the oil companies, the missions, the military, the foreign service, the intelligence community together with the academic world. There are grants and other rewards, there are organizations, there are hierarchies, there are institutes, centers, faculties, departments, all devoted to legitimizing and maintaining the authority of a handful of basic, basically unchanging ideas about Islam, the Orient, and the Arabs.[30]

It was all made to sound conspiratorial ("a pool of interests"), authoritarian ("there are hierarchies"), and corrupt (those "other rewards"). To top it off, the "old boys" were of one hue: "Power in the system (in universities, foundations, and the like) is held almost exclusively by non-Orientals, although the numerical ratio of Oriental to non-Oriental resident professionals does not favor the latter so overwhelmingly."[31]

In 1981, Said published a sequel to *Orientalism*, entitled *Covering Islam*, which expanded on his sketchy indictment of Middle Eastern studies in America and took his argument one step further. The American version of orientalism, he now argued, was even more hegemonic and constricting than its European predecessors. Britain and France had produced a class of "colonial experts" for imperial service,

> but this class did not in turn produce an adjunct to it equivalent to the network of the Middle East studies-government-corporate alliance that exists in the United States. Professors of Arabic or Persian or Islamic institutions did their work in British and French universities; they were called on for advice and even participation by the colonial departments and by private business enterprises; they occasionally held congresses; but they do not seem to have created an independent structure of their own, sustained and even maintained by the private business sector or directly by foundations and the government.[32]

Europe's scholars, Said now decided, "intervened here and there in the conduct of policy, but always after the policy was in place and on the ground so to speak."[33] And however much hostility there was to Islam in Europe, there were always some scholars, like Louis Massignon in France, who displayed "imagination and refinement."[34] Reviewing the works of Rodinson and Hourani, Said announced that "there is no way of imagining how these works might have been produced in the United States," for "in America, unlike Europe, there is both a peculiarly immediate sense of hostility and a coarse, on the whole unnuanced, attitude toward Islam."[35] American scholars were really just drab policy experts in academic disguise; the American academic community simply "responds to what it construes as national and corporate needs."[36] In America, it was a "fact," concluded Said, that "anything said about Islam by a professional scholar is within the sphere of influence of corporations and the government."[37] Throughout *Covering Islam*, "coarse" America was compared unfavorably to "refined" Europe, thus updating the argument of *Orientalism*: bad as orientalism had been in Europe, America made it worse.

Said offered no evidence, no documents, no testimony, and no numbers to substantiate any of his claims about the existence of a "network" of government and academe. He never quantified the "numerical ratio" of "Orientals" to "non-Orientals" in positions of "power" within it. He never bothered to research the precise development of Middle Eastern studies in America. He was ignorant of the debates that had already taken place within the field. He did not even allude to the recent erosion (and near collapse) of external support for these studies. Above all, he failed to make even the most rudimentary distinctions between the center and periphery of the field. Said invested a great deal of energy in other chapters of *Orientalism*. But his treatment of Middle Eastern studies in America was superficial, unsubstantiated, even lazy.

Many failings could be laid at the door of the founders of Middle Eastern studies, but the most damning was their failure to expose the weaknesses of *Orientalism.* A lone (and now-forgotten) rebuttal came from Malcolm Kerr, a political scientist born to two American educators in the hospital of the American University of Beirut, trained at Princeton, and tenured at UCLA. Kerr represented the best in a school that had always seen itself as devoted not only to the pursuit of knowledge, but to the service of the Arab world and its relations with America. Kerr, in his review of *Orientalism* in MESA's journal, expressed a profound disappointment. The book had been

> spoiled by overzealous prosecutorial argument in which Professor Said, in his eagerness to spin too large a web, leaps at conclusions and tries to throw everything but the kitchen sink into a preconceived frame of analysis. In charging the entire tradition of European and American Oriental studies with the sins of reductionism and caricature, he commits precisely the same error.

Kerr (who was not mentioned one way or another in *Orientalism*) determined that the Americans quoted by Said were "not a particularly representative sample of Near Eastern studies in the United States today; and if Said had looked further afield he would have got quite different results." For example, Said omitted any discussion of the many scholars of Arab and Muslim origin who founded and fertilized the field of Middle Eastern studies in America. "Surely as a group," Kerr opined, "they have exerted as much intellectual influence as Said's select roster of ogres, and surely they have not been altogether brainwashed by the tradition." Then there were the numerous American-born scholars, named by Kerr and omitted by Said, whom it would be hard to claim were "bamboozled by the establishment troika of the Zionist lobby, the State Department, and the Ford Foundation." As for scholars who *had* worked for the government or the foundations, "a careful study of their work would indicate consistent *resistance* to the themes of denigration and caricaturization of Eastern peoples of which Said complains."[38]

But Kerr's was a lone voice in American Middle Eastern studies. Bernard Lewis did do battle with Said in the American arena, in an essay on "The Question of Orientalism," published in the *New York Review of Books.* But Lewis was a newcomer to America, and his rebuttal—a vigorous defense of the European tradition—did not take up Said's accusations about the complicities of American Middle Eastern studies. American scholars largely kept silent. Many no doubt thought that Said made certain valid points about anti-Arab and anti-Muslim prejudice that outweighed *Orientalism*'s glaring defects as an account of their field. Others perhaps thought, following Kerr, that Said was "not going to win any races" anyway and that the storm would blow over soon enough. Still others, perhaps more prescient, knew an academic juggernaut when they saw one and simply got out of the way.

But more than anything else, the silence reflected a crisis of self-confidence. The emergence of the Palestinian resistance, the decline of Lebanon into civil war, the rise of the right to power in Israel, and the collapse of the shah not only took most academics by surprise. They cast into doubt the very validity of the modernization and development paradigm that had guided the field. What good were their premises if they could not anticipate the Palestinian explosion, which put Americans in jeopardy across the Middle East? What good were their models, if they could not predict the surge of rage that shut Americans out of Lebanon and Iran, where their presence had been so established and comfortable? The Middle Eastern studies enterprise had not spared the United States even one unpleasant surprise.

The failure arose from the biases of a typically American optimism. But some scholars began to wonder whether they *were* wearing the epistemological blinders which Said called "Orientalism": a contemptuous refusal to see Arabs and Muslims in all their human dynamism. A mix of confusion and guilt had descended on the field even before *Orientalism* came off the presses. Many scholars, far from defending their "guild" (Said's definition), were already predisposed to accept his judgment of their failure: "At almost any given moment during the past few years there has been considerable evidence, available to anyone, that the non-Western world generally and Islam in particular no longer conform to the patterns mapped out by American or European social scientists, Orientalists, and area experts in the immediate postwar years."[39]

The Legacy of *Orientalism*

In the more than twenty years since the publication of *Orientalism*, its impact on the broad intellectual climate in American Middle Eastern studies has been far-reaching. *Orientalism* made it acceptable, even expected, for scholars to spell out their own political commitments as a preface to anything they wrote or did. More than that, it also enshrined an acceptable hierarchy of political commitments, with Palestine at the top, followed by the Arab nation and the Islamic world. They were the long-suffering victims of Western racism, American imperialism, and Israeli Zionism—the three legs of the orientalist stool. Fifteen years after publication of *Orientalism*, the UCLA historian Nikki Keddie (whose work Said had praised in *Covering Islam*) allowed that the book was "important and in many ways positive." But she also thought it had had "some unfortunate consequences":

> I think that there has been a tendency in the Middle East field to adopt the word "orientalism" as a generalized swear-word essentially referring to people who take the "wrong" position on the Arab-Israeli dispute or to people who are judged too "conservative." It has nothing to do with whether they are good or not good in their disciplines. So "orientalism" for many people is a word that substitutes for thought and enables people to dismiss certain scholars and their works. I think that is too bad. It may not have been what Edward Said meant at all, but the term has become a kind of slogan.[40]

The political test included more than "right" and "wrong" in the Arab-Israeli dispute and extended to the entire range of American involvement in the Middle East, about which (and against which) Said offered frequent guidance. The effect of *Orientalism*, as Keddie indicated, was to inspire even more intrusive probes into the political views of scholars. "Unawares perhaps," wrote P. J. Vatikiotis (attacked by Said in *Orientalism*), "Said introduced McCarthyism into Middle Eastern studies—at least in the United States."[41] Rodinson (praised in *Orientalism*) preferred another analogy, describing the book as "a polemic against orientalism written in a style that was a bit Stalinist."[42] Both comparisons pointed to the very same effect.

The analogy to McCarthyism, an American phenomenon, rested upon Said's tendency to list his protagonists and antagonists. Listing was a consistent feature of his style—a favorable reviewer of a later book noted Said's tendency to run together "a string of names, as if that in itself constituted an argument"[43]—and when he listed his orientalists, this effectively became a blacklist. He did it, too, with a combination of incivility and insult. "The guild of the Middle East Orientalists seems to have produced only the likes of Bernard Lewis, Elie Kedourie and the utterly ninth-rate P. J. Vatikiotis," announced Said on one occasion. "These guns-for-hire assure us that Islam is indeed a terrorist religion."[44]

All this went without a collective response. Said, the aggrieved Palestinian, had a license; he was held to a different standard. This indulgence made a telling contrast to the firestorm that broke out in 1984, when two Jewish organizations also named the names of professors whom they identified as propagandists against Israel. In reaction, MESA passed a resolution deploring and condemning blacklists and "false, vague, or unsubstantiated accusations." Scholarly activity, MESA now discovered, required "an atmosphere of academic freedom, open investigation, responsible criticism, and reasoned debate."[45] Ironically, many of those who passed this resolution had already contributed to the deterioration of such an atmosphere, by applauding or acquiescing in the blacklisting style of Said's accusations against their colleagues.

Beyond the overt political allegiance test, *Orientalism* also insinuated an ethnic test for admission to the field. As Keddie noted, the book "could also be used in a dangerous way because it can encourage people to say, 'You Westerners, you can't do our history right, you can't study it right, you really shouldn't be studying it, we are the only ones who can study our own history properly.'"[46] Hourani identified the same problem: "I think all this talk after Edward's book also has a certain danger. There is a certain counter-attack of Muslims, who say nobody understands Islam except themselves."[47]

In a time of limited academic opportunities, *Orientalism* became a valuable tool in ethno-political battles over scarce academic positions. During the 1970s, university budgets were cut, foundations reduced support for area studies, and competition over academic positions grew intense. University graduates from the Middle East did not always find jobs, or failed to land the plum jobs at major centers. As one magazine account noted, the tight job market of the 1970s meant that "some Arab scholars must compete with their American colleagues in order to teach their specialty."[48] Resentments began to simmer, especially against scholars who had landed positions in the boom years.

Orientalism not only overturned bookshelves, it overturned chairs. It became a manifesto of affirmative action for Arab and Muslim scholars and established a negative predisposition toward American (and imported European) scholars. In 1971, only 3.2 percent of Middle East area specialists had been born in the region, and only 16.7 percent had the language and foreign-residence profiles coincident with a Middle Eastern background.[49] "Our membership has changed over the years," announced MESA's president in 1992, "and possibly half is now of Middle Eastern heritage."[50]

Said, of course, preferred to present Middle Eastern studies as a field of ideological triumph. In 1993, he wrote of "the extraordinary change in studies of the Middle East, which when I wrote *Orientalism* were still dominated by an aggressively masculine and condescending ethos."[51] "During the 1980s," he continued, "the formerly conservative Middle East Studies Association underwent an important ideological transformation. . . . What happened in the Middle East Studies Association therefore was a metropolitan story of cultural opposition to Western domination."[52] In fact, so total an "ideological transformation" in MESA (which even named Said an honorary fellow[53]) would not have taken place had there not been a massive shift in the ethnic composition of Middle Eastern studies. In 1988, a younger historian delicately described the mechanism that produced this shift: "Though an ethnic last name does not and should not qualify or disqualify a teacher, my impression is that it is of greater importance to a search committee considering a candidate for a position in modern Middle Eastern history than it would be for a historian of early modern France or Latin American colonial history."[54] A younger political scientist noted "the widespread, if undocumentable, impression that an individual's ethnic background or political persuasion may influence hiring and tenure decisions."[55] For this, Said most certainly did deserve credit. Twenty years after the book appeared, the assembled multitudes of the reconstructed MESA rose from their seats in a standing ovation for Edward Said. Many owed those very seats to *Orientalism*.

In 1981, Said wrote this about Middle Eastern studies (in *Covering Islam*):

> There is no denying that a scholar sitting in Oxford or Boston writes and researches principally, though not exclusively, according to standards, conventions, and expectations shaped by his or her peers, not by the Muslims being studied. This is a truism, perhaps, but it needs emphasis just the same.[56]

The truism remains valid today. But the "standards, conventions, and expectations" have been transformed over the last two decades. In Oxford and Boston and across Middle Eastern studies, they largely conform to those established by Edward Said himself. These scholars, armed with their well-thumbed copies of *Orientalism,* promised to provide real answers to real questions about the real Middle East. Where their orientalist predecessors got it wrong, the post-orientalists would get it right. "Middle Eastern politics are much less unpredictable than is often supposed," announced Roger Owen, a post-orientalist mandarin who personified Saidian dominance in Oxford and Boston. (He taught for a quarter of a century at St. Antony's College, Oxford, before his installation as director of the Center for Middle Eastern Studies at Harvard.) But as Owen himself admitted, "the proof of such an assertion must lie not only in whether or not such an approach is a guide to the present but whether it also stands the test of time."[57] The 1980s and 1990s would put that assertion to the most demanding of tests.

Notes

1. Review of *Orientalism* by Malcolm H. Kerr, *International Journal of Middle East Studies* 12, no. 4 (December 1980), p. 544.

2. Edward W. Said, *The Politics of Dispossession: The Struggle for Palestinian Self-Determination, 1969–1994* (New York: Pantheon Books, 1994), pp. xiii, xv.

3. Rashid I. Khalidi, "Edward W. Said and the American Public Sphere: Speaking Truth to Power," *Boundary 2* 25, no. 2 (Summer 1998), p. 163. The presentation of Said as someone who has regarded the media's attention as "unwelcome," and who would have preferred "the far more congenial tasks of writing and lecturing for smaller audiences on less topical matters," rings false.

4. Edward W. Said, *Orientalism* (New York: Pantheon Books, 1978), pp. 25–28.

5. Ibid., p. 204.

6. Aijaz Ahmad, "*Orientalism* and After: Ambivalence and Metropolitan Location in the Work of Edward Said," in his *In Theory: Classes, Nations, Literatures* (London: Verso, 1992), p. 177. It is ironic that Said should have ridiculed an orientalist for a similarly eclectic display of erudition. Here is Said on Gustave von Grunebaum: "A typical page of his on the Islamic self-image will jam together half-a-dozen references to Islamic texts drawn from as many periods as possible, references as well to Husserl and the pro-Socratics, references to Lévi-Strauss and various American social scientists." Said, *Orientalism*, p. 296. In Kerr's review of *Orientalism* (p. 547), he defined Said's treatment of von Grunebaum as a "summary exercise in character assassination."

7. Interview with Said, *Washington Post,* July 21, 1981.

8. The literature on *Orientalism* is immense. For a summary of various lines of criticism, see Bill Ashcroft and Pal Ahluwalia, *Edward Said: The Paradox of Identity* (London: Routledge, 1999), pp. 74–86.

9. See Bernard Lewis, "The Question of Orientalism," *New York Review of Books*, June 24, 1982. The quote is from Lewis's response to Said, "Orientalism: An Exchange," *New York Review of Books*, August 12, 1982 (this exchange also includes Said's response to the earlier Lewis article).

10. Maxime Rodinson, *Europe and the Mystique of Islam*, trans. Roger Veinus (Seattle: University of Washington Press, 1987), p. 131n3.

11. "'Au-delà de l'Orientalisme': Entretien avec Jacques Berque," *Qantara* 13 (October–November–December 1994), pp. 27–28.

12. William Montgomery Watt, *Muslim-Christian Encounters: Perceptions and Misperceptions* (London: Routledge, 1991), p. 110.

13. Interview with Albert Hourani in *Approaches to the History of the Middle East*, ed. Nancy Elizabeth Gallagher (London: Ithaca Press, 1994), pp. 40–41. Aijaz Ahmad, like Hourani, opined that "when the dust of current literary debates settles, Said's most enduring contribution will be seen as residing neither in *Orientalism*, which is a deeply flawed book, nor in the literary essays which have followed in its wake, but in his work on the Palestine issue." See Ahmad, "*Orientalism* and After," pp. 160–61. It is common for readers of Said to find him most persuasive on subjects with which they are least familiar.

14. David C. Gordon, *Images of the West: Third World Perspectives* (Savage, Md. Rowman and Littlefield, 1989), p. 93.

15. Philip S. Khoury, "Lessons from the Eastern Shore" (1998 Presidential Address), *MESA Bulletin* 33, no. 1 (Summer 1999), p. 5.

16. Clive Dewey, "How the Raj Played Kim's Game," *Times Literary Supplement*, April 17, 1998, p. 10.

17. Said, *Orientalism*, p. 3.

18. A prepublication endorsement by the Marxist cultural theorist Fredric R. Jameson, then a professor of literature at Yale.

19. Interview with Maxime Rodinson in *Approaches*, p. 124.

20. Edward W. Said, *The Question of Palestine* (New York: Times Books, 1979), p. xviii.

21. Lisa Hajjar and Steve Niva, "(Re)Made in the USA: Middle East Studies in the Global Era," *Middle East Report* 7, no. 4 (October–December 1997), pp. 4–5.

22. Said, *Orientalism*, p. 11.

23. Ibid.

24. Ibid., p. 16.

25. Ahmad, "*Orientalism* and After," pp. 195–96.

26. Khoury, "Lessons from the Eastern Shore," p. 2.

27. Said, *Orientalism*, p. 295.

28. Ibid.

29. Ibid., p. 302.

30. Ibid., pp. 301–2.

31. Ibid., p. 324.

32. Edward W. Said, *Covering Islam* (New York: Pantheon Books, 1981), p. 145.

33. Ibid., p. 144.

34. Ibid., p. 12.

35. Edward W. Said, review article in *Arab Studies Quarterly* 2, no. 4 (Fall 1980), pp. 386, 388.

36. Said, *Covering Islam*, p. 145.

37. Ibid., p. 158.

38. Kerr review of *Orientalism*, pp. 544–47.

39. Said, *Covering Islam*, p. 162.

40. Interview with Nikki Keddie in *Approaches*, pp. 144–45.

41. P. J. Vatikiotis, *Among Arabs and Jews: A Personal Experience, 1936–1990* (London: Weidenfeld and Nicolson, 1991), p. 105.

42. Interview with Rodinson in *Approaches*, p. 124. The title of a review by a French journalist, Jean-Pierre Péroncel-Hugoz, suggested yet a third analogy: "Un autodafé pour les Orientalistes," *Le Monde*, October 24, 1980, p. 22.

43. Michael Gorra, "Who Paid the Bills at Mansfield Park? (review of *Culture and Imperialism*)," *New York Times*, February 28, 1993.

44. Edward W. Said, "The Essential Terrorist," in *Blaming the Victims: Spurious Scholarship and the Palestinian Question*, ed. Edward W. Said and Christopher Hitchens (London: Verso, 1988), p. 156. This passage incidentally displayed complete ignorance of Kedourie's formation. Kedourie had prepared an iconoclastic thesis at Oxford, and was *denied* his doctorate by the ostensible master of the "guild," Sir Hamilton Gibb. He became a consistent critic of the "Orientalists"—not of their hostility toward Islam, but of their idealization of it. Said never dealt with Kedourie's ideas; on various occasions, he simply (black)listed him.

45. Resolution passed by members at the MESA Annual Business Meeting, San Francisco, California, November 30, 1984. The resolution was "approved by voice-vote without dissent." See Phebe Marr, "MESA Condemns Blacklisting," *Washington Report on Middle East Affairs*, December 17, 1984. Compare also Karen J. Winkler, "Political Tensions of Arab-Israeli Conflict Put Pressure on Scholars Who Study Middle East," *Chronicle of Higher Education*, March 27, 1985; Naseer H. Aruri, "The Middle East on the U.S. Campus," *Link* 18, no. 2 (May–June 1985), pp. 1–14.

46. Interview with Keddie in *Approaches*, p. 145.

47. Interview with Hourani in ibid., p. 41.

48. "A Scattering of Scholars," *Aramco World* (May–June 1979), p. 22.

49. Richard D. Lambert, *Language and Area Studies Review* (Philadelphia: American Academy of Political and Social Science, October 1973), pp. 47, 59. The 16.7 percent included specialists with at least two visits to the region, total residence of three or more years, one trip since 1964, and one area language skill rated "easily." Many scholars of Middle Eastern background, even if born outside the area, would have met these criteria. Even so, the figure would have included other scholars without any such background.

50. Barbara C. Aswad, "Arab Americans: Those Who Followed Columbus" (1992 Presidential Address), *MESA Bulletin* 27, no. 1 (July 1993), p. 16.

51. Edward W. Said, *Culture and Imperialism* (New York: Alfred A. Knopf, 1993), p. xxvii.

52. Ibid., p. 314.

53. Honorary fellows, of whom there are never more than ten at any one time, are "outstanding internationally recognized scholars who have made major contributions to Middle East studies." http://w3fp.arizona.edu/mesassoc/honoraryfellows.htm

54. Kenneth W. Stein, "The Study of Middle Eastern History in the United States," *Jerusalem Quarterly* 46 (Spring 1988), p. 58.

55. Lisa Anderson, "Policy-Making and Theory Building: American Political Science and the Islamic Middle East," in *Theory, Politics, and the Arab World: Critical Responses*, ed. Hisham Sharabi (New York: Routledge, 1990), p. 54.

56. Said, *Covering Islam*, pp. 17–18.

57. Roger Owen, *State, Power and Politics in the Making of the Modern Middle East* (London: Routledge, 1992), p. 290.

3

Islam Obscured

There are a number of reasons that might explain why Said says nothing about Islam. He might have intended to write only of the West. He might not know enough about Islam. He might have felt that it was sufficient instead to name those of whose work he disapproves. He might have felt it best to say nothing rather than to say some one thing. He might believe that it is inappropriate or impossible or even hostile for any outsider to speak of a belief system which he does not share. Whatever his reason, Said says nothing and says nothing about why he says nothing.

—Leonard Binder (1988)[1]

Said—like the practitioners of "critical scholarship"—had nothing to say about Islam for all these reasons and one more: his academic generation drew upon the experience of the 1960s and 1970s. They were products of late–Cold War third worldism, which they had worked into an epistemology and which could be summarized in three words: resistance, revolution, liberation.

They expected radical change, but of a very specific kind. After 1967, so their argument went, American-engineered schemes for the Middle East could no longer be concealed behind the remote threat of Soviet expansion. Peoples of the region—first and foremost, the Palestinians, followed by other Arabs and Muslims—would rise up against the hegemony of the United States and its clients, especially Israel. There were forces at work, deep in Arab and Muslim societies, which would no longer submit to a skewed order devised solely to preserve American interests.

These forces were progressive. They would not only undermine the old order; they would construct a new order that would raise up and empower the excluded: workers, women, students, intellectuals, refugees. The duty of the sympathetic scholar was to study these forces, prove their potential on a theoretical level, and support them as a practical matter. As the progressive forces seized the initiative in Middle Eastern capitals, their allies would do the same on American campuses.

Blinders and Blind Spots

As an assessment of what had gone before, this analysis was arguable. As a prediction of what was to come, it was lamentable. For as Said prepared the ground for the successful overthrow of the existing order in Middle Eastern studies, in the Middle East itself only Ayatollah Khomeini enjoyed any success in the art of overthrow.

The Achilles heel of *Orientalism*, and much of the "critical scholarship," was its very narrow conception of the forces of change in the Middle East. *Orientalism* made no mention of modern Iran at all, or indeed of any movement framing its agenda in the language of Islam. To Said's mind, it was an orientalist trope to invoke "the return of Islam."[2] "History, politics, and economics do not matter" to the orientalists, wrote Said mockingly. "Islam is Islam, the Orient is the Orient, and please take all your ideas about a left and a right wing, revolutions, and change back to Disneyland."[3] In many contexts, Said insisted upon writing "Islam" with quotation marks, as though it were a category created solely by and for orientalists. That "Islam" might actually serve to mobilize movements more readily than ideologies of left and right seemed not to occur to Said at all. Malcolm Kerr, in his review of *Orientalism*, was struck by the omission: "Does Said realize how insistently Islamic doctrine in its many variants has traditionally proclaimed the applicability of religious standards to all aspects of human life, and the inseparability of man's secular and spiritual destinies? What does he suppose the Ayatollah Khomeini and the Muslim Brotherhood are all about?"[4]

It was a valid question, and one that Said consistently dodged. His *Covering Islam*, published in 1981, represented a scramble to cover the gaping hole in *Orientalism*. Said's indictment of the media and "experts" for their failure to anticipate or explain the revolution in Iran was very much a diversionary tactic, given Said's own failure to do the same in a book published only two years earlier. Nor did he risk offering an interpretation of his own. The closest Said came to an account of Islamism was to blame the orientalists: according to Said, Muslim Orientals, subjected to orientalist demonization, had entered a reactive mode, "acting the part decreed for them" by the experts.[5] By this logic, Said could trace every Islamist excess to Western prejudice, and eventually he did. In 1989, Khomeini issued a *fatwa* (edict) condemning the British-Indian author Salman Rushdie to death for his novel *The Satanic Verses*. "Why is that ignorance there," asked Said, "if not for the disregard, indifference and fear with which things Islamic are considered here? . . . Islam is reduced to terrorism and fundamentalism and now, alas, is seen to be acting accordingly, in the ghastly violence prescribed by Ayatollah Khomeini."[6] This mode of argumentation conveniently absolved Said and followers of the difficult job of accounting for Islamist deeds. Instead, each Islamist action became another opportunity for the repetitive and ritual denunciation of Western prejudice against Islam.

Still, the "return of Islam" was an unwelcome surprise to Said and Saidians. Even more surprising (and, for Said, unpleasant) was the way many Islamist "returnees" read Said's texts. Almost invariably, they understood them as anti-Western, pro-Islamic polemical tracts and deployed them as intellectual ammunition against Islam's "enemies," including secularists in their own societies. By choice or by ignorance, Said had disregarded the prior exist-ence of an elaborate discourse of anti-orientalism within the Muslim world. When these Muslim readers opened *Orientalism* and *Covering Islam,* they per-ceived nothing new, and read them merely as "insider" confirmation of long-standing suspicions that Western scholars *were* agents of their govern-ments, that Western scholarship *was* part of a conspiracy to defame Islam.

In the 1980s, as Iran's revolution resonated abroad, this reading produced some unexpected coincidences. For example, in *Orientalism,* Said determined that American hospitals and universities in the Middle East were tainted by "their specifically imperial character and their support by the United States govern-ment."[7] (Leftists of the MERIP group had leveled the same charge against the American University of Beirut in 1975, describing the university as a "base of operations" funded from Washington and bristling with "sophisticated equip-ment in the field.")[8] It was a telling coincidence that when a militant Islamist movement arose among the Shi'ites of Lebanon in the 1980s, its zealots saw these institutions in just this light and deliberately targeted university and hospi-tal personnel. (By that time, all of these personnel were in Lebanon against the advice of their own government, and had remained there out of sympathy for Lebanese and Palestinians.)

AUB drew much of the fire. In 1982, the university's president became the first American taken hostage in Lebanon. After the abduction, Malcolm Kerr arrived in Beirut to serve as president. Kerr was a son of AUB, a founder and past president of MESA, a supporter of Arab causes—and the lone American critic of Said's *Orientalism.* That he continued to reject Said's premises was obvious from his inaugural address in Beirut. In it, he pointed to the evolution of AUB "from a university offering Western culture to the Arabs, to one that promotes both Western and Arab cultures and implicitly looks for a symbiotic relation between them, in the best tradition of European Orientalism."[9] In 1984, Kerr was gunned down outside his office, by assassins who must have seen this symbiosis and its best tradition as forms of imperialism.

There was much irony in the fact that Said and the "progressive" schol-ars, from the safety of American universities, should have delegitimized the one university in the Arab world where academic freedom had meaning, thanks to its American antecedents.[10] There was irony in the fact that the Beirut hostage-holders of Islamic Jihad should have offered Said's *Covering Islam* as reading to their captive audience of hostages.[11] And there was irony in fact that so many secular intellectuals actually living in the Arab world should have regarded Said's *Orientalism* as a hostile text—ammunition that their Islamist opponents fired off as proof of the innate hostility of the West toward the Muslims.[12]

Islamists surprised Said and followers again in 1989. Rushdie, a novelist with an eye for influential critics, admired Said and shared the professor's political sympathies and antipathies. He also praised Said's courage. "Professor Said periodically receives threats to his safety from the Jewish Defense League in America," said Rushdie in 1986, "and I think it is important for us to appreciate that to be a Palestinian in New York—in many ways *the* Palestinian—is not the easiest of fates."[13] But as it happened, Said's fate became infinitely preferable to Rushdie's, after Khomeini called for Rushdie's death in 1989. It was ironic that Rushdie, a postcolonial literary lion of impeccable left-wing credentials, should have been made by some Muslims into the very personification of orientalist hostility to Islam. Just as ironic was the fact that Said—who had stoked the fires of suspicion in the Muslim world—had read Rushdie's book in manuscript and failed to see the risks in publishing it.[14] There was still more irony in the tendency of some supporters of the death edict to invoke *Orientalism* and *Covering Islam* as evidence for the prosecution—disregarding Said's personal posture of solidarity with the besieged novelist.

Said later admitted that *Orientalism*'s embrace by the Islamists was "the one aspect of the book's reception that I most regret," and that *Orientalism* could "only be read as a defense of Islam by suppressing half of my argument."[15] But Said's surprise at this regular misappropriation of his work underlined his own failure to anticipate Islamism, and the ways it might make him complicit in its sweeping indictment of the West. In fact, it was easy for Islamists to suppress half of his argument because he made it *sotto voce*. In a new introduction to *Covering Islam*, fifteen years after the Iranian revolution inaugurated an era of excess in the name of Islam, the most criticism Said could muster was this: "recourse to a hazy fantasy of seventh-century Mecca as a panacea" was "an unattractive mix that it would be rank hypocrisy to deny."[16] This reservation now stated, Said immediately proceeded to issue new indictments against American scholars and journalists who had tried to say something more. No wonder Islamists so readily discarded this half of his argument: in quantity and style, it seemed insubstantial and *pro forma*.

In sum, Said was repeatedly surprised not only by the force of Islamism, but by the way Islamists recuperated his criticism of orientalism for their own purposes. As this failure of imagination became clearer, Said protested that it was not *his* business to explain any of the messy realities of the Muslim world: "I say explicitly in [*Orientalism*] that I have no interest in, much less capacity for, showing what the true Orient and Islam really are."[17] His job was simply to criticize others. Following his lead, scholars merely repeated stale assurances that kidnappings, hijackings, bombings, and the infamous *fatwa* did not represent Islam—without any explanation of why those Muslims who committed and applauded these acts thought otherwise.

No one outside academe believed that American stereotypes were to blame for the Muslim movements that lived up to them. The expert refusal to narrate left a very wide field to those who would—a handful of scholars and many more journalists who tried to interpret "unattractive" news that came out of parts of the Middle East during the 1980s. Whatever their short-comings, at least this group of commentators did not answer every media query by accusing the media of distortion, or respond to every act of violence against Americans with denunciations of American ignorance and bias.

In the 1980s, the refusal of the academics to move beyond their banalities set the scene for a revealing instance of intellectual poaching. As the Middle East filled front pages, Martin E. Marty, an authority on the history of American Christianity at the University of Chicago, came up with the idea of a project that would compare fundamentalisms. He then retailed this idea to the Chicago-based MacArthur Foundation and the American Academy of Arts and Sciences. Some of the most stimulating studies of Islamism came to be written under these auspices. Predictably, *MERIP Reports* and the *MESA Bulletin* published disdainful critiques of the Fundamentalism Project, but even Said had to acknowledge that the resulting five volumes included "often interesting papers."[18] The Fundamentalism Project conveyed a subtle but powerful message: if the new leaders of Middle Eastern studies persisted in their refusal to address the issue of Islamism head-on, the organizing initiative would come from outside, and the overheads would go elsewhere.

Esposito's Islam

As the 1990s opened, the American public demanded a more substantial interpretation of Islamist movements. That demand was met by an academic entrepreneur who arrived from the far margins of Middle Eastern studies.

During the first part of his career, John L. Esposito never studied or taught at a major Middle East center. He completed a doctorate in Islamic studies at Temple University in 1974 and then spent nearly twenty years teaching comparative religion and Islam at the College of the Holy Cross, a Jesuit college in Massachusetts. His early published work dealt with Pakistan and Muslim family law. Had he continued along this trajectory, he would have remained obscure even by the standards of Middle Eastern studies.

But a fundamental transformation had occurred in the field, opening space at the center for someone positioned at the edge. The rank-and-file of MESA were drawn increasingly from academics like Esposito, at lesser universities and colleges. Many of them were teaching the most basic courses on Islam, with enrollments driven by bad news from the Middle East. They were on the lookout for sympathetic texts on Islam—pitched lower than *Orientalism*, uncontaminated by anti-Americanisms, preferably even written by an American—which they could use in their classes and recommend to their departmental colleagues. Esposito met the demand. In 1984, he published *Islam and Politics*, followed in 1988 by *Islam: The Straight Path*. These were the first of a series of unpretentious, clear, and favorable books on Islam that would become relative best-sellers and go through many editions. In 1988, Esposito was elected president of MESA. Oxford University Press commissioned him to edit a four-volume encyclopedia of the modern Islamic world and seemed content to publish everything else he produced. In 1993, Esposito arrived at Georgetown University, where a Palestinian (Christian) donor endowed a Center for Muslim-Christian Understanding, to support his work.[19] In short order, Esposito assembled a group of like-minded colleagues—two of them, like himself, past presidents of MESA. Grant money began to flow in for conferences and projects. By the mid-1990s, Esposito could claim to speak from the very summit of the field.

Esposito understood that Said's message, despite its immense academic success, carried too much Palestinian, postcolonial, and progressive baggage. To move it beyond the campus, the message needed reformatting, with an ear to the American mainstream. If most of the wider American public respected an argument framed in the language of national interest or moral principles, Esposito would provide it. If most of the American public were amenable to the argument that religion deserved a place in public life, Esposito would make it. If most of the American public were concerned by the possible emergence of "the Islamic threat," he would get them to read his book by titling it *The Islamic Threat*.

This technique owed much to his Muslim mentor. At Temple University, Esposito had prepared his thesis under Ismail R. Faruqi, Palestinian pan-Islamist and theorist of the "Islamization of knowledge," around whom there had developed a personality cult. (Faruqi and his wife were later murdered by an unstable acolyte.) As the years progressed, Faruqi increasingly inhabited a gray zone between scholarship and political activism, his ideals growing ever more radical as he moved through successive stages of Islamist enlightenment. Faruqi opened the world of Islamist activism to Esposito, who was welcomed on Faruqi's recommendation in places as far-flung as Pakistan and Malaysia. Esposito, without choosing Islam, nonetheless became a convert to Faruqi's mission—which, according to the former, consisted of "present[ing] Islam in Western categories to engage his audience as well as to make Islam more comprehensible and respected."[20]

Esposito embraced Faruqi's method. Americans would never understand a presentation of Islam in its own categories—that would take more knowledge and empathy than most students, journalists, and officials could be expected to muster. But they might see Islam and Islamist movements more favorably, were they presented in Western categories. Fundamentalism was one such category, but it had strong pejorative associations, more likely to excite suspicion than respect. Why not place Islamist movements in the political category of participation, or even democratization?

The popularity of this idea within the field had roots in a widespread frustration. While other parts of the world democratized through the 1980s, the Muslim Middle East did not. While experts on Latin America, Eastern Europe, and Russia went off to advise new governments on the mechanics of democratic transition, the experts on the Middle East stayed home. Kings and presidents-for-life would not be moved; the most visible opposition movements called for an Islamic state. The Middle East looked like an exception, at a moment when "exceptionalism" was being denounced as an orientalist thought-crime.

To resolve this anomaly, Esposito came forward to claim that Islamist movements were nothing other than movements of democratic reform. Only orientalist prejudice, of the kind dissected by Said, prevented American observers from seeing past external form to this inner quality. Americans would "have to transcend their narrow, ethnocentric conceptualization of democracy" to comprehend "Islamic democracy that might create effective systems of popular participation, though unlike the Westminster model or the American system."[21] This idea—that Americans suffered from an ethnocentric understanding of democracy—soon reverberated throughout Middle Eastern studies. Historian Richard Bulliet, on-and-off director of the Middle East Institute at Columbia University (and self-described "consultant to the Department of State")[22] declared (in a Washington conference) that the defining of democracy was part of "a world hegemonic discourse of Western cultural imperialism." He urged "the reshaping of the concept of democracy within world terms in which there is a dialogue of discourse and not simply a Western hegemonic discourse."[23]

Armed with this indictment of American ethnocentrism, academic experts could now assert that every Islamist state or movement was either democratic or potentially democratic. Historian John Voll, Esposito's closest collaborator (whom Esposito would bring to Georgetown from another remote outpost, the University of New Hampshire) appeared before a congressional committee in 1992, where he pleaded on behalf of Sudan—a place without political parties, ruled by a military junta in league with an Islamist ideologue. Voll described the Sudanese regime as "an effort to create a consensual rather than a conflict format for popular political participation," and then delivered this opinion: "It is not possible, even using exclusively Western political experience as basis for definition, to state that if a system does not have two parties, it is not democratic."[24] And so American congressmen were instructed by the president-elect of MESA that a country with no political parties, presided over by a coup-plotting general, ridden by civil war, with a per capita gross domestic product of $200, still might qualify somehow as a democracy. This was not deliberate self-parody; it was merely Esposito's logic advanced *ad absurdum.*

As for Islamist violence, this was deemed beyond the bounds of approved research. Dwelling upon it would only reinforce stereotypes. After all, announced Esposito, "most" Islamic movements had reached the conclusion that violence was "counterproductive." "They speak of the need to prepare people for an Islamic order rather than to impose it."[25] Therefore, promised Esposito, the violence that had marred the 1980s would recede, and "the nineties will prove to be a decade of new alliances and alignments in which the Islamic movements will challenge rather than threaten their societies and the West."[26]

Yet despite these assurances, there seemed to be no shortage in the 1990s of Islamists still prepared to live up to orientalist expectations. Acolytes of shaykhs angry at America continued to plant massive bombs—inside the World Trade Center in New York, near an American barracks in al-Khobar, outside American embassies in Nairobi and Dar Es Salaam. Tourists in Luxor, bus riders in Tel Aviv, and pedestrians in Algiers all became the targets of lethal and indiscriminate attacks. Not all of the Islamists—perhaps not even "most" of them—had heard that violence was "counterproductive."

Whenever such an act occurred, scholars who had promised a waning of the violence entered a state of denial. After the World Trade Center bombing, Columbia's Richard Bulliet organized a conference—not to explain the appearance of terrorism in his city, but to confront "a new anti-Semitism" against Muslims, driven by "the propensities of the non-elite news media to over-publicize, hype, and sell hostility to Islam." These media were the real fanatics. "Some Muslims from New York are going to be tried for seditious conspiracy to commit criminal acts," he warned ominously. "A guilty verdict will send a chill of fear throughout America."[27]

This was typical of the hyperbole popularized by Said—and it was just as misplaced. When "some Muslims" eventually were found guilty, there was no chill of fear, and no new anti-Semitism. Americans, in their basic fairness and respect for due process, saw the bombing trial as a straightforward criminal case. In their coverage of the arrests and trial, "non-elite" journalists and commentators again outperformed the tabloid academics, who had been indoctrinated by Said to expect only the worst from America beyond the campus.

From the Islamists, these same scholars expected only the best. Islamists were either moderate or moderating, moving steadily toward a rational accommodation with changing reality. The Palestinian Hamas was a case in point. In 1993, *Foreign Affairs* opened its pages to Bulliet, who considered the "possibility that a Hamas campaign of violence could cause the Rabin government to fall and return the Likud Party to power." Given the track record of Hamas, this did look like a cause for concern. "But that outcome seems unlikely," Bulliet reassured his readers, "since it would amount to Israel playing into the hands of the spoilers. Violence, therefore, will probably be deemed too great a risk by Hamas leaders."[28] The prophet did prophesy falsely: two years later, a violent campaign of suicide bombings by Hamas did return the Likud to power, with implications for the balance of the decade. Academics blinded by the paradigms of Said and Esposito continued to be surprised not only by America, where they lived, but by the Middle East, which they studied. Still, the expectations of their academic milieu remained very predictable, and as long as they met them, they remained safe and secure behind its impenetrable defenses.

Muslim Luthers

Were there any Muslim activists who deserved to be explained, and not just explained away? Yes: the leading lights in the "Islamic reformation."

The idea of "Islamic reformation" perfectly fit the agenda of presenting Islam in Western categories. It first surfaced in journalistic usage. "Islam is now at a pivotal and profound moment of evolution," wrote the journalist Robin Wright in 1992, "a juncture increasingly equated with the Protestant Reformation."[29] Islam was experiencing "a new spirit of reform," she wrote in 1993, "addressing some of the same issues—such as the relationship between church and state—central to the 16th-century Christian Reformation."[30] "The reformers' impact is not merely academic," she wrote in 1996. "By stimulating some of the most profound debate since Islam's emergence in the seventh century, they are laying the foundations for an Islamic Reformation."[31]

The analogy received academic legitimacy two years later. It came not from Esposito, whose base within a Jesuit-run institution effectively ruled out his deployment of the Reformation trope. Instead it came from Dale Eickelman, a Dartmouth anthropologist. "If my suspicion is correct," he wrote in an article entitled "Inside the Islamic Reformation," "we will look back on the latter half of the twentieth century as a time of change as profound for the Muslim world as the Protestant Reformation was for Christendom."[32] This was exciting news for the practitioners of Middle Eastern studies, who were frustrated by the sheer persistence of old leaders, old orders, and old conflicts. Now they, too—so they persuaded themselves—were witnessing the most important moments in Islam since its revelation, or at least (in Bulliet's words) "the most exciting period in Islamic religious history since the twelfth century."[33]

Did Eickelman and others realize that the heralding of an "Islamic reformation" echoed a classic orientalist trope? Nearly forty years ago, the political scientist Manfred Halpern criticized orientalists "because they often sympathetically, but perhaps with Christian parochialism no less than forbearance, await a Moslem reconsideration of Islamic theology as a sign of an Islamic

Reformation and hence neglect the social and political revolution that instead is under way."[34] A. L. Tibawi, an earlier (Muslim) critic of orientalist scholarship, also writing nearly forty years ago, was genuinely offended. "Orientalists, and more particularly those who are Protestants, cannot free themselves from what might be called the inevitability of the Reformation," he complained. Western anticipation of a Protestant-like reformation insinuated what earlier Western polemicists openly denounced as Islam's "falsehoods" and "defects."[35] "Orientalists mask their distaste for their subject by calling for reform," observed MERIP's indictment of Middle Eastern studies twenty years later. "Islam needs a thoroughgoing Reformation of its own in order to gain vitality and meaning," to exit a state of "weakness, inadequacy, and stagnation."[36] The resort to the Reformation comparison in the 1990s was but one more example of how academics kept recycling old analogies, probably without even being aware of it.

But for the Reformation analogy to be persuasive, there had to be identifiable reformers. A major project of Middle Eastern studies in the 1990s thus became the quest for a thinker who would nail his theses to the mosque door. In the early 1990s, the searchers fixed upon Rashid al-Ghannushi, an exiled Tunisian philosophy teacher and leader of that country's Islamist movement, in whose writings some heard an echo of support for pluralism. Ghannushi once spent six months speaking and travelling in the United States, and Esposito, for one, pinned high hopes on him.[37] Something of the exalted reputation of Ghannushi in academic circles was conveyed by a course description of an offering on democratic theory at Tufts University, where students would examine the thought of "Ghannoushi, Habermas, Havel, Huntington, Jefferson, Madison."[38] But on closer listening, one could also hear disturbing echoes in Ghannushi's line, especially his fierce denunciations of conspiracies by "Jewish Masonic Zionist atheistic gangs," and his expressions of support for some of the least accommodating Islamists.[39] This kind of rhetoric tended to obscure whatever innovation could be detected in his writings.

In the mid-1990s, the spotlight fell upon the Tehran University philosopher Abdolkarim Soroush, a disillusioned son in the revolution. "Supporters and critics now call him the Martin Luther of Islam," gushed Robin Wright, "a man whose ideas on religion and democracy could bridge the chasm between Muslim societies and the rest of the world."[40] Soroush was an American academic's dream, who mixed his Islamic sources with citations from Hume and Kant, Kuhn and Popper. The enthusiasm of the academics even got him an article in *Time*. ("He has the West paying attention, too," the magazine confided. "The Council on Foreign Relations in New York recently issued a 56-page study devoted to Soroush's political thought.")[41] Most American academics got a chance to hear the philosopher on one of his American lecture tours. But Soroush (whose courage was undeniable) did not appear to have a substantial following in Iran, where few people beyond university campuses understood his obtuse method of reconciling disparate thought.

In the late 1990s, the mantle briefly settled upon the shoulders of Muhammad Shahrur, a Syrian civil engineer who had published an 800-page tract on the Qur'an in 1990. "A publishing event is sweeping the Middle East," enthused Eickelman in a 1993 piece for the *MESA Bulletin*. "From the Arab Gulf to Morocco a modernist, not to say liberal, interpretation of the Qur'an by a Syrian civil engineer who interprets his own scriptures has become a best-seller." Shahrur's 800-page tome was an appeal for the application of human reason to the Qur'an, much in the spirit of the "Islamization of knowledge." Eickelman suggested the book might be "an intellectual equivalent in the Arab world to Allan Bloom's *The Closing of the American Mind*." [42] But five years later, he offered a far more ambitious analogy: "Shahrur's book may one day be seen as a Muslim equivalent of the 95 Theses that Martin Luther nailed to the door of the Wittenberg Castle church in 1517." [43] In 1998, Eickelman brought Shahrur to Chicago, where he was unveiled before an assembled MESA conference. Few were impressed.

It is a recurring theme: the Western sympathizer sets out for the East in search of a Muslim thinker, who is then presented to Western audiences as forerunner of a great reformation. The English poet-explorer Wilfrid Scawen Blunt, the Victorian enthusiast for Islam, set the first precedent more than a century ago, when he announced that the ideas of Jamal al-Din "al-Afghani," the Iranian activist and philosopher, "stood in close analogy to what we have seen of the re-awakening of the Christian intellect during the fifteenth and sixteenth centuries in Europe." [44] Afghani once allowed one of his admirers to introduce him to a London audience with these words: "He is the Luther of the new Reformation, and I trust that he will persuade the English people to move their Government in our favour." [45]

Each of the Muslim Luthers of the 1990s was seized upon and discarded by American enthusiasts in rapid succession, as it became clear that none of them could "deliver," at least not in the ways expected by their foreign admirers. Traditional Muslims were bound to reject them, believing like Tibawi that "perceptible 'reform' cannot be effected in the doctrines of the faith without diminishing or canceling their validity." [46] Nontraditional Muslims did not need them either. "Secularization is already a *de facto* reality," wrote one of them, the Moroccan scholar Abdou Filali-Ansari, even though "the equivalent of the Christian Reformation" was "far from having been achieved." [47] But rather than focus upon that *de facto* reality, America's Middle East experts remained obsessed with a handful of Muslim "thinkers," who were debating issues in principle that had been resolved in practice.

The reality of secularization owed nothing to the Muslim thinkers paraded on American lecture tours. It owed everything to the state. Muslim liberalism "still has many voices, some of them very creative and of consider-

able talent," historian Aziz Al-Azmeh acknowledged, "but the most important [one] is the Arab state, which has embraced Islamic modernism as its
own."[48] American academics, by their preoccupation with would-be Luthers,
succumbed to the occupational hazard of overestimating the role of intellectuals. And by discounting the state, they failed to discern the deeper
processes of state-generated and state-sanctioned secularization that had
expanded the scope for social change, and would block the ascent of Islamism
to power.

Vested Interests

By the end of the 1990s, Islamism seemed less like the dawn of a new age and
more like a lunge for power that had failed. It was a Frenchman, Olivier Roy,
who as early as 1994 had the courage to publish a book entitled *The Failure of
Political Islam* and to write of the Middle East as having entered the stage of
"post-Islamism."[49]

But few in the United States had any interest in concurring; for while
political Islam may have failed in the Middle East, it had been a spectacular
success in American academe. The high profile it had conferred upon certain scholars had produced tenure, grants, book contracts, and even
directorships of centers. Yvonne Haddad, another MESA president stabled
at Esposito's center, admitted that "since 1979 many members of MESA have
had a meteoric rise in their careers." One of her colleagues confided to her
"that if someone were tracking his achievements he should have a stamp
engraved on his forehead reading 'Made by Khomeini.'"[50] "Islam *has* become the center of political and moral discourse throughout the Islamic
world," announced Columbia's Bulliet, adding: "Right prediction, it seems,
has its rewards."[51]

In a paradoxical way, these academics needed the "clash of civilizations."
Strife sustained the flow of rewards. After all, it was now their responsibility
to sustain the institutions of Middle Eastern studies that they had seized.
How many resources within the university could they command if their
phones stopped ringing and their deans did not see and hear them quoted
in the national newspapers and on public radio? And how would enrollments hold up if Muslim movements failed to hit the headlines? When Bulliet
at Columbia taught "The History of Islamic Society, from Muhammad to the
20th Century," or Voll at Georgetown taught "Islam and the West," were they
not banking on the eternal appeal of the orientalist cliché? Who needed
reified Islam now?

"For the foreseeable future," predicted Esposito in 1997, "the conditions
and issues that have spawned Islamic revivalism and political Islam will continue. . . . [U]nderstanding the nature, record, and potential impact of
political Islam is more critical than ever."[52] "I see no reason to suspect that
the appeal of political Islam, in some form, will lessen in the coming years,"

Bulliet told a Washington conference in 1998. Quite the opposite: Islamic politics, he announced, would "become increasingly important in our pondering of American policies toward the Islamic world."[53] These were plausible arguments—but only if terrorists like Osama bin Laden were included under the rubric of political Islam. After all, the edicts of bin Laden, not the tomes of the "reformers," had the most "potential impact" on America and its policies.

But in the 1990s, as in the 1980s, the academics refused to study those very Muslims whose radical interpretations of Islam put them on a collision course with America. Bin Laden was a case in point. The academics were so preoccupied with "Muslim Martin Luthers" that they never got around to producing a single serious analysis of bin Laden and his indictment of America.[54] Bin Laden's actions, statements, and videos were an embarrassment to academics who had assured Americans that "political Islam" was retreating from confrontation. If they mentioned bin Laden at all, it was to dismiss his influence. "Focusing on Osama bin Laden," wrote Esposito in 1998, "risk[s] catapulting one of many sources of terrorism to center stage, distorting both the diverse international sources (state and nonstate, non-Muslim and Muslim) of terrorism as well as the significance of a single individual."[55] Potential sources of terrorism may have been diverse, but there could be no doubt by 1998 which source had the most "potential impact" on America, and which source was most likely to seize "center stage."

And so while the academics brooded over the "diversity" of terrorist threats, it was left to journalists and terrorism experts to follow the bin Laden trail and predict the dangerous trajectory of his school of political Islam. The academics then protested against the worrisome conclusions of other experts and dismissed the warning signs. "The threat of terrorism has spawned a big industry, and has struck fear and horror in the American psyche," complained Sarah Lawrence professor Fawaz Gerges, whose book on U.S. policy toward Islamic movements was inspired by the Esposito paradigm.

> Should not observers and academics keep skeptical about the U.S. government's assessment of the terrorist threat? To what extent do terrorist "experts" indirectly perpetuate this irrational fear of terrorism by focusing too much on farfetched horrible scenarios? Does the terrorist industry, consciously or unconsciously, exaggerate the nature and degree of the terrorist threat to American citizens?[56]

It was easy to envision multitudes of academics nodding in agreement. Gerges published his complaint exactly six months before terrorists brought down the World Trade Center.

In retrospect, the new elite in Middle Eastern studies had failed to ask the right questions, at the right times, about Islamism. They underestimated its impact in the 1980s; they misrepresented its role in the early 1990s; and they glossed over its growing potential for terrorism against America in the late 1990s. Twenty years of denial had produced mostly banalities about American bias and ignorance, and fantasies about Islamists as democratizers and reformers. These contributed to the public complacency about terrorism that ultimately left the United States vulnerable to "surprise" attack by Islamists. But there was no serious debate over Islamism within the field itself. Middle Eastern studies were so heavily invested in one interpretation that few dared to challenge the collective migration from one error to another. Dissent could be found only in think tanks that encouraged it, and in the Middle East itself, among intellectuals with a nearer and more acute angle of vision on Islamism in practice.

Even before the catastrophe of September 11, 2001, some portions of the general public had begun to write off academic "expertise" on political Islam. The loss of public confidence reflected the yawning gap between the actual conduct of Islamist movements and their representation by the academy. The camp led by Esposito assured America that "most Islamic movements are not necessarily anti-Western, anti-American, or anti-democratic."[57] But as an exasperated Gerges admitted, "time and again, Islamists have proven to be their own worst enemies" by "being equivocal about democratic norms, human rights, peaceful relations with the West, and the use of terror in the pursuit of domestic political goals."[58] Most Americans could tell that the professors were engaged in special pleading, a suspicion confirmed by the countless discrepancies between academic punditry and Islamist word and deed.

How long would it take for this failure to register within the academy? The academics—remote from the Middle East, distant from Washington, accountable to no one—could probably muddle through another decade without a reckoning. As long as they engaged in the ritual of condemning the public, the media, and the government for ignorance of Islam, they could be reasonably assured of the solidarity of their guild. But by the middle of the 1990s, the contraction of Islamist movements had left a vacuum in Middle Eastern studies. What would fill it? Salvation seemed to reside in the discovery of "civil society." The result would be yet another lavishly funded intellectual failure, on a scale only America could afford.

Notes

1. Leonard Binder, *Islamic Liberalism: A Critique of Development Ideologies* (Chicago: University of Chicago Press, 1988), pp. 120–21.

2. Edward W. Said, *Orientalism* (New York: Pantheon Books, 1978), pp. 107, 225, 316.

3. Ibid., p. 107.

4. Review of *Orientalism* by Malcolm H. Kerr, *International Journal of Middle East Studies* 12, no. 4 (December 1980), p. 545.

5. Edward W. Said, *Covering Islam* (New York: Pantheon Books, 1981), pp. 52–53. "Not that there really is not an Islamic revival independent of the reactive process." There was—

but to Said, it was not clear whether the terms "Islam" or "Islamic" did justice to its diversity.

6. Lisa Appignanesi and Sara Maitland, eds., *The Rushdie File* (Syracuse: Syracuse University Press, 1990), p. 165.

7. Said, *Orientalism*, p. 294.

8. [Peter Johnson and Judith Tucker], "Middle East Studies Network in the United States," *MERIP Reports* 38 (1975), p. 15.

9. "Inaugural Address of President Malcolm H. Kerr," December 3, 1982, *AUB Bulletin* 25, no. 4 (December 13, 1982).

10. Another irony was to follow, for at an opportune moment Said completely reversed his view of the American universities in the Middle East. "The modern American university seems the last utopian place," he told an interviewer in 1997, "a liberal ideal that has helped the Middle East, in its manifestations in Cairo and Beirut." See "Conversations with Outstanding Americans: Edward Said," *Christian Science Monitor*, May 27, 1997. The reassessment was timely. In 1999, Said collected an honorary doctorate from the American University in Cairo, and was received enthusiastically by a crowd of 1,000 at the American University of Beirut. "The atmosphere was almost like a carnival," reported the Beirut *Daily Star* (July 7, 1999).

11. "A few English books were brought for us to read," recalled Rev. Benjamin Weir, one of the hostages of Islamic Jihad. "In one way or another they all centered on topics the guards thought we ought to know. Some of the books were about the Iranian revolution, others about the history and development of Shiite religious thought. One book, by a Columbia University professor, dealt with the misunderstanding of Islam in the West." Benjamin and Carol Weir (with Dennis Benson), *Hostage Bound, Hostage Free* (Philadelphia: Westminster Press, 1987), p. 156. More specifically: "There became available a few books in English, provided not only for our recreational interest but presumably for our education. There was Edward Said's *Covering Islam*." See Benjamin M. Weir, "Reflections of a Former Hostage on Causes of Terrorism," *Arab Studies Quarterly* 9, no. 2 (Spring 1987), p. 157.

12. See in particular the criticism of Said by the Syrian philosopher Sadiq Jalal al-Azm, "Orientalism and Orientalism in Reverse," *Khamsin* 8 (1981), pp. 5–26.

13. Salman Rushdie, "On Palestinian Identity: A Conversation with Edward Said," in his *Imaginary Homelands: Essays and Criticism, 1981–1991* (London: Granta Books, 1991), p. 171.

14. Said read the book in typescript. "He didn't anticipate what Khomeini would do," said Said of Rushdie. "My impression was he was expecting the novel to have an impact. He said it would shake up the Muslims. But he never expected it to bring about a threat to his life." See W. J. Weatherby, *Salman Rushdie: Sentenced to Death* (New York: Carroll and Graf, 1990), p. 108. Nowhere does Said say he himself thought that publication of the text might endanger Rushdie.

15. Afterword to 1994 edition of Said, *Orientalism*, pp. 330, 332.

16. Introduction to 1997 Vintage Books edition of Said, *Covering Islam*, p. xv.

17. Afterword to 1994 edition of Said, *Orientalism*, p. 331.

18. Introduction to 1997 Vintage Books edition of Said, *Covering Islam*, p. xvii.

19. John L. Esposito, "A Man and His Vision," in *Hasib Sabbagh: From Palestinian Refugee to Citizen of the World*, ed. Mary Jane Deeb and Mary E. King (Washington, D.C.: The

Middle East Institute, 1996), pp. 71–82. "Georgetown University declined requests for exact funding information," reported a sympathetic news item in 1996. Eleanor Kennelly, "Catholic Georgetown Mecca for Islamic Study," *Metropolitan Times*, February 7, 1996.

20. *Encyclopedia of the Modern Islamic World*, s.v. "Faruqi, Isma'il al-Raji" (John L. Esposito).

21. John O. Voll and John L. Esposito, "Islam's Democratic Essence," *Middle East Quarterly* 1, no. 3 (September 1994), p. 11.

22. Bio in Timothy D. Sisk, *Islam and Democracy: Religion, Politics, and Power in the Middle East* (Washington, D.C.: United States Institute of Peace, 1992), p. 84.

23. Quoted in ibid., p. 59.

24. Hearing statement of John Voll, May 20, 1992, Subcommittee on Africa of the Committee on Foreign Affairs, House of Representatives, *Islamic Fundamentalism in Africa and Implications for U.S. Policy* (Washington, D.C.: Government Printing Office, 1993), pp. 65–72.

25. John L. Esposito, *The Islamic Threat: Myth or Reality?* (New York: Oxford University Press, 1992), p. 166.

26. Ibid., p. 207.

27. Richard W. Bulliet, "Rhetoric, Discourse, and the Future of Hope," in *Under Siege: Islam and Democracy*, ed. Richard W. Bulliet (New York: Middle East Institute of Columbia University, 1994), pp. 4, 7.

28. Richard W. Bulliet, "The Future of the Islamic Movement," *Foreign Affairs* 72, no. 5 (November–December 1993), p. 43.

29. Robin Wright, "Islam, Democracy, and the West," *Foreign Affairs* 71, no. 3 (Summer 1992), p. 133.

30. Robin Wright, "Muslims Open Up to Modern World," *Los Angeles Times*, April 6, 1993.

31. Robin Wright, "Islam and Liberal Democracy: Two Visions of Reformation," *Journal of Democracy* 7, no. 2 (April 1996), p. 64.

32. Dale F. Eickelman, "Inside the Islamic Reformation," *Wilson Quarterly* 22, no. 1 (Winter 1998), p. 82.

33. Bulliet, quoted in Sisk, *Islam and Democracy*, p. 60.

34. Manfred Halpern, "Middle Eastern Studies: A Review of the State of the Field with a Few Examples," *World Politics*, 15, no. 1 (October 1962), p. 116.

35. A. L. Tibawi, "English-Speaking Orientalists: A Critique of Their Approach to Islam and Arab Nationalism: Part 1," *Islamic Quarterly* 8, nos. 1–2 (January–June 1964), p. 41; idem, "Second Critique of English-Speaking Orientalists and Their Approach to Islam and the Arabs," *Islamic Quarterly* 23, no. 1 (January–March 1979), p. 6. The notion of an "Islamic reformation" was simply "another attempt to change the Muslim view of Islam, and to bring it as near as possible to Christianity, or, better still, to the Protestant form of Christianity."

36. [Johnson and Tucker], "Middle East Studies Network," p. 20.

37. "Symposium: Resurgent Islam in the Middle East," *Middle East Policy* 3, no. 2 (1994), pp. 15–16.

38. Course on "The Future of Democracy," offered by the Tufts University Education for Public Inquiry and International Citizenship, http://msanews.mynet.net/MSANEWS/199701/19970121.9.html

39. All these themes recur at length in an interview by Intra*View*, February 10, 1998, http://msanews.mynet.net/Scholars/Ghannoushi/

40. Robin Wright, "Islam's Theory of Relativity," *Los Angeles Times*, January 27, 1995.

41. Scott Macleod, "Democracy vs. the Ayatullahs: Abdelkarim Soroush Challenges Iran's Regime," *Time*, June 23, 1997. The reference is to the report by Valla Vakili, "Debating Religion and Politics in Iran: The Political Thought of Abdolkarim Soroush," Council on Foreign Relations, January 1996.

42. Dale Eickelman, "Islamic Liberalism Strikes Back," *MESA Bulletin* 27, no. 2 (December 1993), p. 167.

43. Eickelman, "Inside the Islamic Reformation," p. 84.

44. Wilfrid Scawen Blunt, *Secret History of the English Occupation of Egypt* (London: Unwin 1907), p. 102.

45. Quoted in Nikki R. Keddie, *Sayyid Jamal ad-Din "al-Afghani": A Political Biography* (Berkeley: University of California Press, 1972), p. 359.

46. Tibawi, "English-Speaking Orientalists," p. 42.

47. Abdou Filali-Ansari, "Islam and Secularism," in *Islam, Modernism and the West*, ed. Gema Martín Muñoz (London: I.B. Tauris, 1999), pp. 133–34.

48. Aziz Al-Azmeh, *Islam and Modernities* (London: Verso, 1993), p. 33.

49. Olivier Roy, *The Failure of Political Islam*, trans. Carol Volk (Cambridge: Harvard University Press, 1994).

50. Yvonne Y. Haddad, "Middle East Area Studies: Current Concerns and Future Directions" (1990 Presidential Address), *MESA Bulletin* 25, no. 1 (July 1991), pp. 1–2.

51. Richard W. Bulliet, "Twenty Years of Islamic Politics," *Middle East Journal* 53, no. 2 (Spring 1999), p. 190.

52. John L. Esposito, "Introduction," in *Political Islam: Revolution, Radicalism, or Reform?* ed. John L. Esposito (Boulder: Lynne Rienner: 1997), p. 13.

53. Bulliet, "Twenty Years of Islamic Politics," p. 195. This was the keynote speech presented at the annual conference of the Middle East Institute.

54. For the lone (and telling) exception, see Bernard Lewis, "License to Kill: Usama bin Ladin's Declaration of Jihad," *Foreign Affairs* 77, no. 6 (November/December 1998), pp. 14–19.

55. Esposito added mention of bin Laden to the third edition of his book, *The Islamic Threat: Myth or Reality?* Full text at http://msanews.mynet.net/books/threat/6.11.html

56. Fawaz A. Gerges, "The Ultimate Terrorist: Myth or Reality?" *Daily Star* (Beirut), March 12, 2001. His book: *America and Political Islam: Clash of Cultures or Clash of Interests?* (Cambridge: Cambridge University Press, 1999).

57. Esposito, *The Islamic Threat*, p. 212.

58. Gerges, *America and Political Islam*, pp. 241–42.

4

Misstating the State

Today there is a broad empirical consensus among Western and Middle Eastern scholars about political conditions in the Middle East. They agree that states are weak and, as their economic crises grow worse, getting weaker. They concur that the weakness of the state partly reflects and partly encourages greater assertiveness by social groups: while the states are paralyzed, movements like the Islamists appear to have seized the initiative. Some think the growing energy of social groups can be harnessed to help forge democracies in the region.

—*Yahya Sadowski (1993)*[1]

As the 1990s drew to a close, it became abundantly clear that "social groups" had not changed the course of Middle Eastern history. That course continued to be set by the Middle Eastern state. The state, far from being paralyzed by the Islamist challenge, emerged hardened and strengthened by the test of its mettle. And no democracies had been forged by the "energy" of other "social groups." The resilience of the state should have surprised no keen observer. But in America's seats of Middle Eastern studies, among the upholders of the "broad empirical consensus," this came as a rude shock—and a cruel disappointment.

At one time, of course, many of these same academics had been ardent believers in the state—back when it adhered to "progressive" values like revolution and socialism, which some of them shared. Elizabeth and Robert Fernea, later pillars of the Middle East center at the University of Texas, headed off to Cairo in mid-1959. "We have a chance to see Egypt in the process of building a new nation, a chance to witness revolutionary change first hand," Robert told a doubting colleague. "We would sit on the Victorian porch of the old Semiramis Hotel, beside President Nasser's new riverside Corniche," the couple later reflected. "And while we contemplated the eternal Nile, we felt that we were truly fortunate to be in Egypt at this time. The river, black and gleaming by night, remained the same, but Egypt was changing: an ancient nation was being reborn, we believed, awakening from years of domination by others to assume responsibility for its own destiny."[2]

61

Roger Owen, the Oxford don later imported by Harvard, confessed to the spell cast by five-year plans over his generation of Western academics:

> We grew up to be complicit with what we took to be the progressive state-building enterprises of the early post-colonial independence period. Living as I did in Cairo in the early 1960s, it was difficult not to become excited by the Nasser project, to see Egypt—and perhaps the rest of the world—through his eyes, to write about it using the same highly charged vocabulary of planning and education and social justice for all. Even now, when so much about that period has been revealed as hollow and flawed, it still requires an effort to resist the old bright shiny words or to see Arab society from any other vantage point than Cairo or Damascus or Amman.[3]

Damascus and Amman were places that Cairo planned to bring under the one umbrella of an Arab superstate. This idea, too, had its enthusiasts among the foreign scholars. Michael Hudson, a political scientist and later director of the Center for Contemporary Arab Studies at Georgetown, was one of them:

> July 14, 1958—Jubilant crowds of young men are surging through the Hamidiyyah suk in Damascus. One of them explains breathlessly to an American student standing nearby that the Western puppet monarchy in neighboring Iraq has just been overthrown. Another obstacle to Arab unity has given way. . . . Anyone introduced to Arab politics at that particular moment, as I was, carries a lasting image of nationalist enthusiasm that seemed destined to erase "artificial" borders and unify a national community too long and wrongly divided.[4]

But by the mid-1960s, it was hard to deny the repressive nature of the military regimes of Egypt and other Arab countries, or to expect much of Arab unity. The United Arab Republic, which linked Egypt and Syria in 1958, broke apart in 1961. In 1964, the Ferneas overheard people in Cairo speaking "of the secret police, of the torture of dissidents, of long incarceration of political prisoners in faraway oasis prisons."[5] After 1967, it was self-evident that Nasser and his imitators had not only failed to effect a revolution; they had led their peoples to a ruinous defeat.

Understating the State

But in the early 1970s, a younger generation of leftist scholars began to insist that the "bright shiny words" of revolution be taken seriously again—not when uttered by leaders in Cairo, Damascus, or Amman, but when pronounced by the Palestinian movement and its sympathizers. The decisive defeat of Arab states in 1967 had led them to write off not only Nasser, but all of the existing regimes. Drawing on the precedent of 1948, they assumed that defeat would overturn the status quo in the Arab world, and they pinned their hopes on the Palestinian movement as the new vanguard of Arab revolution. These "progressive" scholars dismissed the conservative power of states and their armies, and hailed the revolutionary power of fedayeen on rock-strewn hills.

The Palestinian camps in Jordan became places of pilgrimage for Arab-Americans who later became important figures in the field. Hisham Sharabi, professor of history at Georgetown, visited Jordan in the summer of 1969 and wrote a study amplifying the exaggerated claims of the fedayeen. (The Jordanian security forces had been "won over by the guerrillas," he wrote. They could be suppressed "only if outside forces intervene in some form or another.")[6] "I was in Amman during the summer of 1969 and then again in 1970," wrote Edward Said. "I was a visitor but also an exhilarated participant in the national revival that I saw taking place."[7] The exhilaration was not limited to Palestinians. Philip Khoury, a future president of MESA, spent an undergraduate year abroad at AUB in 1969–70. "I believed that the [Palestinian] Resistance was the future," he later recalled, and he too visited the camps in Jordan in the summer of 1970.[8]

But despite the defeat of the Arab states on the battlefield, they remained masters of the art of survival. After all, most Arab leaders had come to power by coup, and they knew exactly what it took to nip opposition in the bud. Unlike the defeat of 1948 which inaugurated a bout of instability, the even more humiliating defeat of 1967 marked the beginning of an era of unprecedented stability, even immobility. As for the Palestinian "revolutionaries," they were driven out of Jordan in 1970 and allowed a small space in the weakest of the Arab states, Lebanon, where they were contained and corrupted.

Among the "progressive" scholars, the disappointment was palpable. In 1971, Edward Said expressed astonishment that "King Hussein, the Baathists in Iraq and Syria, President Sadat, the Lebanese and Saudis—essentially the same organs of power *personally* (in some cases) present and responsible for the immense Arab defeat of 1967—are still visible exactly as they were four years ago."[9] Said refused to believe that these wily old plotters had managed this trick on their own, and (as usual) laid the blame at the door of America:

> Hitherto little-known studies done in universities or by the RAND Corporation, the Hudson Institute, or agencies of the Department of Defense enabled the United States to outmaneuver the Palestinian guerrillas by using, and financing, all the governments in the area who stood to lose most if the Palestinians were to have fulfilled their revolutionary role.[10]

The notion that Arab regimes were merely puppets "dangling from all-too-obvious strings" (Said's characterization) simply postponed any serious analysis of their durability.

The traumatic loss of Lebanon also biased a generation of American scholars, who reflexively predicted disintegration of Arab states and regimes at the slightest sign of trouble. American scholars, from their perch at AUB, had seen an Arab state come completely undone, with very little warning. Many of them now overreacted, becoming doomsayers who saw only omens of collapse and chaos.

One of them was Michael Hudson who spent time in Lebanon during the early 1960s and had published a prescient book on the country entitled *The Precarious Republic* (1968). There he rightly determined that "the loads on this system [are] increasing even faster than its capabilities," and that Lebanon's political future would be "stormy."[11] Hudson got it right at a time when many American observers predicted smooth sailing for Lebanon.

Alas, Lebanon became Hudson's template for the entire Arab world, and over the next quarter-century he emerged as a predictable pessimist about the prospects of virtually every Arab state and regime. In his 1977 book *Arab Politics: The Search for Legitimacy,* he announced that "the future of systems which rely mainly on traditional legitimacy [i.e., monarchies] is not bright, notwithstanding their unexpected durability." As for "the legitimacy potential of the revolutionary systems" (i.e., republics), it was "still seriously marred by the intractability of the participation problem."[12] This pessimism persisted into the 1980s, by which time Hudson had become director of Georgetown's Center for Contemporary Arab Studies. In 1985, he wrote an essay (for a conference on "The Coming Arab Decade") anticipating state-society relations in the Arab world of the 1990s—a text that perfectly summarized "expert" consensus on where the Arab state was headed in the decade to come.

Hudson envisioned three possible scenarios: a continuation of the status quo ("rulers rule, people obey"); an "era of turbulence" ("marked by instability and incoherence"); and an "era of legitimacy" (in which "a social contract or constitution—rather than absolutism or anarchy—are the principal structures"). Which of these would prevail? "One is persuaded to predict change of some sort rather than the status quo," concluded Hudson. "From observation of contemporary Arab politics, one is prompted to suppose that, on the whole, the factors supporting the status quo are not so powerful as those which generate change." And lest anyone conclude that this view rested only upon observation, Hudson insisted that "this judgment rests, first, on a theoretical perception of state and society in the Arab world that sees society as capable of nurturing significant political forces independent of the state."[13]

True, admitted Hudson, these states had powerful security services. But these were "not likely to be decisive because of the limitations imposed by 'underdeveloped' administration, communications and the like." True, opposition groups appeared to be in disarray. But "they may be now at a state in which their 'learning curve' (their ability to absorb technical and organizational innovation) is ascending, while that of regimes and their security bureaucracies remains flatter." And true, the United States cemented the existing Arab order. But "American patronage also exerts a 'kiss of death' effect on friendly Arab regimes by virtue of the United States' larger Middle East policy concerns."[14] Hudson could not decide which was more likely, an "era of turbulence" or an "era of legitimacy." But he left no doubt as to his own skepticism about the sustainability of the status quo.

Rashid Khalidi went even further than Hudson in his own essay on "The Shape of Inter-Arab Politics in 1995" (prepared for the same 1985 conference). Supremely confident of his powers of prediction, Khalidi (arriving in America after a decade of teaching in Beirut) promised not to hide behind what he called "a smokescreen of scenarios." "[T]he pattern of superficial stability which has prevailed in the Arab world for the past 15 years will surely change," he announced, "perhaps radically." That change had a predetermined timeframe, and Khalidi was bold "to suggest unequivocally that this current pattern will not, indeed cannot, continue for another decade." Like Hudson, he had decided that "many of the factors which have contributed to both stability and prosperity are disappearing or have disappeared." The inescapable conclusion: "There will undoubtedly be changes of rulers, and probably changes of regime." And as a result of these domestic upheavals, the inter-Arab system could "be expected to change dramatically by 1995."[15]

These were not prophets in the wilderness. They came from the very heart of the American Middle Eastern studies establishment. Hudson became president of the Middle East Studies Association in 1986; Khalidi became president in 1993. But for all of Hudson's formidable powers of "observation" and his acute "theoretical perception," and for all of Khalidi's self-assurance ("surely," "unequivocally," "undoubtedly"), no new "era" commenced by 1995, the expiration date of their essays. The Arab world instead continued to conform almost perfectly to Hudson's own description of the (least likely) status quo scenario: in the monarchies, skillful manipulation and peaceful transitions; in the big states, successful appeasement of key clienteles and decisive deployment of strong security measures.

The failure to understand the play between state and society came most vividly to the fore at midpoint in the "coming Arab decade," after Iraq invaded Kuwait in 1990. The Gulf War provided a once-in-a-generation opportunity for academic Middle East "experts" to reach a wide audience, and to justify their claim to privileged understanding. In practice, many of them could not push past their own emotions and commitments, leaving former diplomats and military experts to fill the demand for dispassionate analysis. Still, there were a few subjects on which Middle East "experts" were deemed especially competent. No one reasonably expected them to second-guess Saddam Husayn, but if these "experts" were just that, they should have been able to say accurate things about the position of Saddam Husayn within Iraq, the resolve of the Iraqi army, and the response of Arab opinion in the Middle East generally. All of these questions ultimately turned upon an intimate understanding of the complex interaction of Arab state and society.

During the crisis, Rashid Khalidi emerged as one of the most influential commentators from within Middle Eastern studies. By this time, he had established himself as associate director of the Middle East center at the University of Chicago, which gave his assessments particular resonance. Khalidi could have been expected to emphasize the Palestinian dimension of the crisis (and perhaps even excused for doing so). But in every assessment of what major actors would or would not do, he erred.

Would a war coalition built partly on Arab foundations hold if the United States refused to criticize Israel while building it? "I don't think the coalition can withstand this sort of double standard by the United States. It's a weak link."[16] (Wrong: the coalition held right through the campaign, although the United States deferred all Arab-Israeli issues to the aftermath.) Would the Iraqi army fight? "They're in concrete bunkers. And it won't be easy to force them out without resorting to bloody hand-to-hand combat. It's my guess that they'll fight and fight hard, even if you bomb them with B-52s."[17] (Wrong: the Iraqi army collapsed, American forces were greeted by waves of surrendering Iraqi soldiers.) After the defeat, would Saddam be able to keep his grip on power? "The Baath has everything at stake. It could go down with the ship. At some point, it might decide that its interests are not inextricably tied to Saddam Hussein and that, in order to placate external powers who would favor the stability of a strong Baath party without Saddam, they might ditch him."[18] (Wrong again: the Ba'ath party decided nothing in Iraqi politics, Saddam wielded it as a tool which remains, even ten years later, utterly subservient to his will.)

In 1994, in a "Presidential Letter" issued to members of MESA, Khalidi made no apologies. Despite the dismal failure of his short-term predictions of 1990–91, and the near expiration of his mega-prediction of 1985, he could still lament how often "the consensus of experts in the Middle East field on a given matter is ignored by leaders and governments in framing their policies (which then sadly often result in disaster)."[19] Of course, that policymakers might have *avoided* disaster by *ignoring* "expert" consensus remained a possibility that "expert" consensus could never allow.

Inventing Civil Society

The real disappointment was that the Arab masses had not used the opportunity of Saddam's bold stroke to rise up against their oppressive rulers. The Gulf War instead restored the status quo in Kuwait and reinforced the old order elsewhere. But the pundits continued to issue earthquake warnings.

Hisham Sharabi had no doubts about the catharsis to come:

> What you have now is a few ruling elites who have privileges and power, and who are either totally isolated from their people, or potentially at cross-purposes with their people. This is why I say the potential for destabilization, for radical transformation, though totally unforeseeable in terms of specific modalities, is to my mind—unlike in the aftermath of 1967—inevitable.[20]

According to Hudson, the anti-American demonstrations that preceded the war in some Arab capitals were the first gusts of a storm:

> People say the street didn't rise up. In fact, the street did rise up all across North Africa and Jordan, Yemen, and in places where the street might have risen up if there hadn't been such strong internal security pressure, you would have seen more than you saw. I think a great deal of damage has been done to the American position among the people of this area, particularly in Arab and Islamic opinion. I think there is a lot to worry about there.[21]

But these were only premonitions, bereft of any conceptual framework. To make this sort of prediction persuasive, it needed more elaborate theoretical trappings—a logic proving that society *had* to trump the state. There had been a false start in 1987, when the Social Science Research Council in New York launched a Middle East project with the confident title: "Retreating States and Expanding Societies." The project soon sputtered to a halt: predicated on nothing real, it produced nothing real, and it lacked a savvy academic entrepreneur. But a few years later, just such a figure did appear: Augustus Richard Norton.

Norton's arrival from the margins of Middle Eastern studies bore a resemblance to Esposito's. A decorated Vietnam veteran, career army officer, and graduate of the University of Miami, Norton received some training in Arabic at the Defense Language Institute in Monterey, before being seconded to United Nations operations in south Lebanon in 1980. He was perhaps the last American whose Lebanese experience provided material for a doctorate, which he wrote at the University of Chicago. Norton then taught political science at West Point, on the farthest edge of the field.

By the 1980s, career military service was hardly a credential for an enthusiastic reception in Middle Eastern studies. But Norton's message, like Esposito's, precisely served the agenda of the new establishment in Middle Eastern studies, which needed an emissary to spread its gospel of imminent change. Colonel Norton knew how to appear before a congressional committee. And he knew how to write an op-ed piece framed in the language of national interest. But he was also willing to make the necessary bows to orthodoxy, to affirm his own "intolerance for essentialism,"[22] and to deride "the influential denizens of Orientalism."[23]

His timing was impeccable. The Middle East never loomed larger for Americans than it did in the aftermath of the Iraqi invasion of Kuwait and the Gulf War. The war provided a short-term windfall for academics—most of whom sank right back into obscurity once the dust had settled. But a few political scientists realized that the massive media attention lavished on the Middle East had primed the major foundations, opening new opportunities—provided the right hook could be found. Norton found it, in the form of "civil society." In early 1992, the Ford Foundation launched an ambitious initiative to track down "Civil Society in the Middle East," and Norton came to New York University to direct it.

Norton drew upon Hudson's earlier thesis, but amplified it. "The region's governments," he announced, "especially the Arab ones, face a persistent crisis of legitimacy."[24] (This notion of a "persistent crisis" defied the customary definition of crisis as a decisive moment or turning point. Most Arab governments were actually in a state of persistent stasis and had not faced a domestic crisis in years.) The theme of crisis returned in the title of a 1994 article (coauthored with journalist Robin Wright): "The Post-Peace Crisis in the Middle East." Here Norton looked forward with certainty (and transparent anticipation) to "the next phase of Middle East upheaval," the "impending turmoil": conflict would pit "societies against their governments," the former represented by "burgeoning forces of change."[25] The notion of an "acceleration" of the "crisis" appeared again that same year, in Norton's introduction to the collected volumes generated by his project: "The [Gulf] war certainly accelerated the crisis by highlighting the inefficiency and weakness of many of the regimes." "The Middle East after the Arab-Israeli conflict," he wrote, "will experience an acceleration in domestic political crises."[26] Norton amplified this message via all the means afforded by the project: a newsletter, a film, and two volumes of published papers, preceded by numerous deliberations. ("Meeting in a spot like the Villa Serbelloni in Bellagio, Italy, generates excitement amongst participants," he wrote.)[27]

But the "upheaval," the "turmoil," and the "crises" never materialized. The Gulf War did not accelerate the demise of any regime, even Saddam Husayn's. The regimes parried the Islamist thrust, and nothing fundamental changed in the domestic politics of countries at peace with Israel. Obviously the regimes had resources and strengths that were not visible from the veranda of the Villa Serbelloni. Rulers were allied to elites, groups, sects, families, and tribes whose members had a strong, vested interest in the status quo and who were determined to do whatever they deemed necessary to preserve it. Beneath the massive inefficiencies of the state, very efficient security services ferreted out opponents of the existing order. Many of the rulers, especially monarchs whose claims rested upon a combination of genealogy and Islam, enjoyed a legitimacy invisible to outsiders but omnipresent for their subjects.

By 1996, even Norton had downgraded his "crisis" to a "severe challenge," and acknowledged that "the regimes have proven to be remarkably durable and highly resistant to pressures for profound political and economic reform."[28] By 1999, "acceleration" had disappeared altogether from Norton's lexicon; now the state was "slowly retreating." "The slow retreat of authoritarianism is under way," he wrote, clinging to the last straw of optimism.[29] In fact, it was the political scientists, led by Norton, who were beating their own slow retreat. "Civil Society Strikes Back," announced an article generated by the ill-conceived Social Science Research Council project.[30] To the contrary: in the 1990s, "civil society" struck out.

By the second half of the 1990s, many American political scientists understood this, but most of them were thoroughly invested in the paradigm. How could it be salvaged? Faced with bankruptcy, the "civil society" theorists pleaded for a U.S. government bailout, urging American intervention to shift the domestic balance of power in the Middle East. "To be on the right side of history and political reform in the Middle East," announced Norton, "the West may occasionally have to confront even some of its key allies."[31] "Governments may require nudging and pushing in the direction of dialogue by major powers," he wrote elsewhere. "And outside powers will have to guarantee internal processes of reform and be prepared to stifle meddling by recalcitrant authoritarian governments like Saudi Arabia."[32]

This was the advice of someone who billed himself as an "occasional consultant" to the State Department and the National Security Council.[33] To judge from U.S. policy, those occasions must have been few and far between. But Norton's priority lay first and foremost with salvaging the "civil society" paradigm, even if it meant summoning the *deus ex machina* of American power—and this, precisely on behalf of those in the Middle East who were the most hostile to American power.

The United States did no such thing, and as the 1990s closed, doubts began to surface even within the guild. An early admission that things had gone wrong came from none other than Michael Hudson. In a 1996 article, he continued to argue that regimes lacked legitimacy. But he also admitted that every Arab experiment in democratization had failed, leaving a "lack of fit between theoretical expectations and empirical realities." One empirical reality: "The state apparatus remains large and pervasive, and regimes continue to hold a powerful advantage over opposition parties. The *mukhabarat* [security-intelligence] state may be retreating a bit, but it still stands as a formidable obstacle to democratization." Since "we seem to have underestimated the durability of authoritarianism," Hudson admitted, he now found it appropriate to ask "whether we were guilty of misplaced ideological optimism, flawed theoretical assumptions, or some combination of the two."[34]

Another disillusioned political scientist, James Bill, found the right metaphor to describe the obsessive behavior of his colleagues, who clung to their paradigm in the face of all evidence. "American analysts continue to explore their political empty quarter," he wrote in 1996,

> in search of the oases of knowledge necessary to explain political development in the Middle East. Eventually, these analysts all seem to end up at the same old watering holes, believing they have discovered new oases and giving them different names each time. In the 1950s and 1960s, the signs at the oases read "liberal democracy and Westernization"; in the 1960s and 1970s, the search focused on "political development and political participation"; in the 1970s and 1980s, the jargon was "legitimacy" and "the state and society" dichotomy; today, the words on the weather-beaten old signs are "civil society" and "democratization." We have come full circle.[35]

If this were so, then the migrating tribe of political scientists would always return to some form of the "civil society" paradigm. For the "civil society" paradigm in America drew upon an ethos embedded in the deepest strata of culture—in this instance, American culture generally, and its academic subculture specifically. Missionary drive, an activist disposition, and can-do optimism infused the attempt to apply the "civil society" paradigm to the Middle East. This was political activism, not political science. Indeed, it was not too far-fetched to describe this activism as America's indigenous orientalism: a closed epistemological circle, postulating the corrupted state of the Muslim East, which might only be alleviated through the beneficent intervention of American power.

The Palestinian Exception

While the Arab world generally disappointed the "civil society" theorists, they placed great store in the prospects for Palestinian democracy. The Palestinians had always been the "chosen people" of Middle Eastern studies in America. After 1967, they alone had stood up to Israel, assaulting Israel's borders with little more than rifles. In 1982, in Lebanon, they had delayed the advance of the Israeli war machine more effectively than any Arab army. After 1987, they had risen up against Israeli occupation—with simple stones.

They not only fought with more effect. They also were believed to have a vibrant "civil society," both inside and outside Palestine. They had representative institutions, unions, and associations. Their leaders were accountable. Allow them self-rule, and the Palestinians would prove that the Arab world could sustain democracy. Perhaps the Palestinian example would even democratize the Arab world, as Yasir Arafat suggested in an interview in the mid-1980s:

> In our mini-state our democracy will be a model which many Arab peoples will want to copy. Then perhaps they will demand the democracy that we Palestinians are enjoying. And how will the regimes react to that? There is

no doubt the regimes are frightened of our democracy. Perhaps that is the number-one cause of many of our problems in the Arab world.[36]

In American academe, the notion that the Palestinian movement was the exception to the Arab rule had a long history. The Georgetown team of Hudson and Sharabi championed the idea. "Compared to many of the Arab systems," wrote Hudson in his *Arab Politics* (1977), "the Palestinian polity did not have a serious legitimacy problem."[37] "Unlike most of the established regimes, the government of the Palestinians rested not on coercive capabilities, which were very limited, but on the legitimacy which most Palestinians freely accorded it."[38] Sharabi went still further: "For anyone familiar with the facts," he wrote, "the uniqueness of the PLO lies not in its 'terrorism' but in the kind of democracy it practises. The Palestinians, despite their dispossession and dispersion, exercise today probably one of the few functioning democracies in the Third World."[39]

But it was Edward Said, in his *Question of Palestine* (1979), who made the most detailed and extravagant claims for Palestinian democracy. Fatah? "Fateh tacitly encourages a real democracy in political idea and style."[40] The Palestine Liberation Organization? "I myself am greatly impressed with the generous presence in the PLO of values, ideas, open debate, revolutionary initiative—human intangibles whose role, I think, has far exceeded, and has commanded more loyalty than the routine organization of a militant party might have."[41] The Palestinian National Council? "For the first time in recent memory there was a broadly representative national body in the Arab world actually debating important matters in a totally democratic way. . . . There is no Arab country in which such things can go on, in which the leadership's accountability is searched and its responsibility gone over openly, discussed, analyzed, resolved upon in an orderly way."[42]

There remained the problem of Arafat, whose presence loomed over the PLO. "Fateh's (and indeed Arafat's) models are basically Nasserite," Said admitted in *The Question of Palestine.* But he then suggested that Arafat was a figurehead, a "visible symbol of authority—the *za'im,* Arafat, also known as 'the old man,' whose mere continuous presence guarantees the existence of the Palestinian cause." This "much misunderstood and maligned political personality"—only a "symbol of authority," not authority itself—exercised his leadership "without at the same time ever appearing to be despotic or capricious."[43]

What, then, was the nature of political authority in the Palestinian movement? Said offered this account: "Exiled Palestinians contribute regularly to the Palestinian National Fund (PNF). Like all Palestinian agencies, including the PLO itself, the PNF is accountable to the Palestinian National Council, which fulfills the function of a parliament or legislative branch." The budget thus created "has grown to the extent that it effectively pays for services, supplies, training, and armaments for approximately a million people." Yes, money also came in from the Arab states, but it did not represent the bulk of the budget: "Supplementing the money voluntarily given by Palestinians has been an annually fluctuating sum garnered from various Arab states."[44] And Said brushed off reports of irregularities in the PLO's operation: "If at times the PLO seemed to be chaotic in its overall business, that too was in part a function of its peculiar genius for conscripting Palestinians from many directions at once."[45]

Taken together, then, Said's PLO was truly exceptional in the Arab world: a democratic government led by a symbolic figurehead, financially accountable to a representative parliament for funds offered voluntarily by common people. Here was a kind of legitimacy no Arab government could approximate, and no Palestinian rival could challenge. Said confidently determined that "there is not the remotest chance that any alternative Palestinian leadership will ever emerge; the PLO is too legitimate and representative a body for that to happen."[46]

By the mid-1980s, a few observers began to point to cracks in the edifice built so assiduously for Americans by Said and followers. Rashid Khalidi stopped well short of questioning the judgment of Arafat, and his few criticisms of the PLO were buried in a 1986 book justifying PLO decisionmaking during the siege of Beirut. But even those few criticisms were telling. For example, Said had claimed that the PLO was financially accountable to representative Palestinian institutions. But as Rashid Khalidi admitted (in a footnote), there was no transparency whatsoever in PLO finances: "There are no reliable figures on PLO finances: all published estimates on its budget are based on speculation. This is an area where a large measure of secrecy has been maintained."[47] Said had written that the funds provided services for a million people. But massive budgets had also gone to salaries paid directly to a few tens of thousands of loyalists. Khalidi acknowledged that "this wealth seriously corrupted the ideals and practices of the PLO itself, turning many of its cadres into employees."[48]

The corruption did not begin or end at the level of cadres. The acquisitiveness of some leaders had been so manifest during the PLO's Beirut years that Khalidi could not but mention "the spectacle of individual Palestinian officials who had grown rich, or had obtained a luxurious apartment, expensive car, and armed bodyguards because of their involvement with the PLO."[49] Jean Genet, the French playwright and besotted admirer of the Palestinian revolution, described this corruption with literary flair in his posthumous *Prisoner of Love* (1986), a narrative of his Palestinian sojourns:

> It took me several years to realize how some of the leaders—well-known ones whose names are mentioned in Western newspapers—became dollar millionaires. It was tacitly known or half-known that the seas of the Resis-

tance had thrown up not a few bits of flotsam and jetsam but a whole strong-box in which each of them had one or more drawers containing proofs of his fortune in Switzerland or elsewhere. Each knew what the others had, too, because their fortunes were often the result of a division of the spoils.[50]

Genet concluded that "there were always sharks among the leaders who instead of hijacking aircraft hijacked the Resistance's funds. Some Palestinians, very ordinary people, cited evidence to me, named names, and were full of contempt for Arafat's entourage."[51]

And what of the "real democracy" of the PLO, hailed by Said and Sharabi? The operations of the Palestinian National Council (of which Said was a member from 1977 until 1991) largely served to justify the claim to democracy. But as Khalidi allowed, "the formal structures of the PLO were rarely the forums for crisis decisions, and most PLO decisions had to be made in times of crisis."[52] Nor did the PLO Executive Committee, elected by the PNC, live up to its name: "Far from being the seat of real executive power, in practice it resembled nothing more than an unwieldy and weak coalition government with little control over vital matters." Khalidi located "real power" in the "top ranks" of Fatah.[53]

And in those "top ranks," one opinion counted more than all the others combined. British journalist Alan Hart, author of a fawning 1984 biography of Arafat ("definitive," according to Khalidi; "the best informed, most detailed account of Arafat that I have seen," according to Hudson)—noted that Arafat "is, many of his colleagues say, more of a dictator than a democrat."[54]

In short, the exiled Palestinian "government" (Hudson used the term even in the 1970s) did not differ in kind from the Arab regimes around it. The leaders, formed by their experience in Cairo, Amman, Beirut, and Tunis, sought to duplicate the Arab model. Genet discerned this already in the mid-1980s: "Like Algeria and other countries that forgot the revolution in the Arab world, my Palestine thought only of the territory out of which a twenty-second [Arab] state might be born, bringing with it the law and order expected of a newcomer."[55]

Yet no one in Middle Eastern studies could proclaim this, for a simple reason: Edward Said had not yet proclaimed it. It would be difficult to underestimate how effectively Said defined the boundaries of acceptable discourse on Palestinian aspirations and the PLO for American academe. By the 1980s, no other academic authority could dare challenge him on Palestinian ground. And for Said, the PLO remained, right through the 1980s, "an inspiring movement for freedom and justice, across national divisions, boundaries, and language."[56] The PLO's exceptional character remained an article of faith until Said resigned his membership in the PNC in 1991—the moment when "for the first time in two decades I realized that I had no faith in the leadership of the organization I had previously supported."[57] According to Said, it was only then, "in the 1990s," that the PLO became "a quasi-official Arab state organization, not unlike, indeed far too much resembling, the bureaucracies and dictatorships it was forced to deal with in the region."[58]

This was an astonishingly belated discovery by Said. By the time he wrote his 1994 epilogue to *The Politics of Dispossession*, Said's indictment of the PLO had grown rhetorically rich: "Why should hard-pressed Palestinians in refugee camps in Lebanon and Gaza accept corruption, Parisian shopping sprees, and continued bumbling among a handful of officials directed from Tunis?"[59] But had the PLO been free of corruption, Parisian shopping sprees, and official bumbling *before* Said's 1991 resignation? In his writings from the mid-1990s, "Said reveals how very early on he had become disenchanted with the PLO leadership"—so wrote two of his acolytes, by way of praise.[60] But the corollary of this statement was that, from very early on, Said *concealed* his disenchantment with the PLO leadership. Indeed, even when he resigned his PNC membership in 1991, he concealed the principal reason, adducing only reasons of health. "I said not one word more, and because (against hope) I wanted our efforts to succeed I didn't criticize what I felt was a tragically mistaken policy."[61] As it happened, the wider American public did not have to await Said's epiphany to know that the PLO already conducted itself like an Arab state, and that Arafat ran it with a high hand. They had Thomas Friedman's *From Beirut to Jerusalem* (1989), which was full of telling vignettes that pointed in just this direction.[62] But in academe, *The Question of Palestine* still limited what could be said about diaspora Palestinian politics to banalities about the PLO's broad inclusiveness.

"Democratic Palestine"

The *intifada*, the Palestinian uprising in the West Bank and Gaza that began in 1987, extended this idealization to Palestinian politics in the Israeli-occupied territories. In the furnace of the uprising, declared the political scientists, the Palestinians of the West Bank and Gaza had forged their own vibrant "civil society."

By the early 1990s, a good deal of the "civil society" rhetoric hinged upon the West Bank and Gaza. In the absence of a state, the Palestinians had organized themselves in unions and associations, all of them seemingly nongovernmental. While the rest of the Arab world suffered from personalized rule, the Palestinians of the West Bank had built a political life based upon institutions. Here was fertile ground for the creation of an Arab democracy.

Sharabi refined his gospel of Palestinian exceptionalism at a Georgetown conference convened to mark (and even celebrate) the *intifada*. "The Palestinians have it in their power, if they consciously so decide, to build a true democracy in the Arab world," he announced. A high rate of literacy; the many universities and hospitals; the unions of workers, women, and students together constituted "the makings for an exemplary free and democratic state" and a "living example" to an Arab world threatened by "new forms of despotic structure." The *intifada* embodied human rights, civil rights, and self-determination, and if "democratic liberties can be realized in the Palestinian state, what will prevent their realization across the Arab world?"[63]

It was not only Palestinian-born scholars who insisted upon the Palestinian exception, now centered on the West Bank and Gaza. William Quandt listed the reasons why "Palestinians care about democracy." They had had "bad experiences with authoritarian Arab regimes." They had been "influenced by the political life of their closest neighbors, Israel and Jordan." And above all, during the *intifada* they had "acquired the habits of participating in political life, wielding authority, making decisions, and not always deferring to the *diktats* of the Tunis-based PLO."[64]

Academics who were disillusioned by the Palestinian "outside" now had the option of idealizing the Palestinian "inside." Glenn Robinson, author of a book on Palestinian state building, presented the Palestinians of the West Bank and Gaza as accomplished practitioners of democracy. "Palestinian civil society has been perhaps the most active and vibrant in the Arab world," he determined. "During the *intifada*, the individuals and institutions active in civil society formed what can only be called a protostate," whose "authority was pluralistic, and even democratic, in its decision making."[65] The most important of these institutions were the nongovernmental organizations (NGOs), which "represent the core of resistance politics under occupation."[66] Scholars who failed to acknowledge the existence of this "dynamic and pluralistic civil society" were guilty of "an essentialist, antidemocratic understanding of Arab-Islamic political culture."[67]

But Palestinian "civil society," it became clear during the 1990s, was not sufficiently "vibrant" or "dynamic" to check the excesses of Palestinian authoritarianism. The Palestinian Authority, established on Arafat's return to the West Bank and Gaza in 1994, did not deviate significantly from the prevailing Arab norm. The leader made himself the subject of a personality cult and concentrated power in his own hands. Competing security services, a dozen in number, intimidated the opposition, reined in the NGOs, and muzzled the press. Corruption took root, and the sale of monopolies hobbled the economy. None of this met with effective resistance from "civil society." The situation was marginally better than the Arab norm, thanks in large measure to watchdogs positioned by international donors. But this did not suffice to make the new Palestinian polity a clear exception to the prevailing rule.

Paradoxically, in Palestine itself, astute observers offered explanations of the kind no one in American academe dared to offer, precisely because they invoked the banished concept of political culture. "There is no tradition of accountability in the Palestinian national movement," wrote Ziad Abu-Amr, a professor of political science at Birzeit University and a member of the Palestine Legislative Council. "A powerful indigenous culture has prevailed over new influences and historic traumas," so that Palestinian political culture "remains highly traditional, patriarchal, and parochial." Even the "sociopolitical pluralism" of the Palestinians was "less a matter of principle than an extension of the variety that marks the world of tribal or familial relations." In sum, concluded Abu-Amr, "Palestinian political culture is far from being 'civic.'"[68]

Ahmad S. Khalidi, a Palestinian academic based in Britain, later described the myth of Palestinian exceptionalism as the triumph of image over substance:

> No matter what image the Palestinians have of themselves—in particular the carefully cultivated self-image of the large and vociferous Palestinian intelligentsia—the truth is that Palestinian society in its basic structure and orientation is fundamentally no different from the Arab societies that surround it.

Palestinian society, like other Arab societies, was "still dominated by traditional rural modes of action and behavior, still motivated by local differences and tribal rivalries, and still marked by conflicts of class and clan." Democracy? It was "a tradition that has no real antecedents either within the Palestinian polity itself or the Arab world." Those who believed otherwise were "either naïve or ill-informed." As for the Palestinian Authority (PA), Khalidi found nothing "surprising" in the "conformity of the Palestinian system to the Middle Eastern norm."[69]

But the American academics did profess surprise. How could they not? They had come under the total domination of the Palestinian professorate in America, who had justified the Palestinian cause by claiming that its triumph would produce the first Arab democracy. When it did not, the disappointment ran deep. "The PA has become an authoritarian polity run by a despot," lamented Glenn Robinson. "For those people who have followed Palestinian politics over the years, such a political outcome is both sad and surprising."[70] Sad it may have been, but surprising? Two decades of pro-Palestinian activism, Saidian indoctrination, and politically correct self-censorship, had combined to create unsustainable expectations in American academe. Elizabeth and Robert Fernea once wrote that the Palestinians "were overlooked and underestimated in the 1950s and 1960s by American social scientists."[71] This was true enough, but in the 1970s and 1980s they were idealized and overestimated. This was just as serious a failing, but no one (yet) had the courage to admit it.

Misreading Israel

If there was one place in the Middle East where the state did shrink, and "civil society" did gain at its expense, it was Israel. Economic liberalization, privatization, deregulation, electoral reform, media proliferation—by each process, the state retreated still further from society and the economy. This crucial change took the new establishment in Middle Eastern studies by complete surprise. Blinded by ideology, they continued to invoke the antiquated paradigm of Israel as a colonial garrison state, even as Israel moved in the opposite direction.

Joel Beinin, one of MERIP's guiding spirits and a historian at Stanford, belonged to this group, and personified its narrow vision. For the 1988 volume on *The Next Arab Decade*, Beinin provided the "insider" forecast on Israel. The title of the article defined Israel as a "garrison state." Its economy had entered into a "deep crisis" because of the burdens of military expenditure. Israel's economy had been "massively reoriented toward military requirements," and Beinin expected military production "to dominate Israel's industrial and export economy." What about civilian hi-tech? "There have been recent efforts to build up high-technology exports in Israel," Beinin noted dismissively, "but the development of technology is often linked to military applications." Militarized to the hilt, Israel might even be approaching a dead end: "The economic crisis in Israel could easily get out of control, and a total economic collapse is not inconceivable."[72]

The supremely confident Beinin then delivered a prophecy which he did not bother to hedge:

> In the coming decade, we can expect to see a series of crises in the Israeli economy, sharpening social and political conflict, a more aggressive stance toward the Arab world, and growing Israeli dependency on the United States. This analysis suggests a pessimistic assessment of the likelihood that any government which will come to power in the foreseeable future will seek to resolve the Arab-Israeli conflict on terms which will secure self-determination for the Palestinian people.[73]

It did not even take a full ten years to prove Beinin wrong in every particular. In the decade following publication of his grim forecast, Israel's economy doubled in size; Israel became a global center for civilian hi-tech; military industries retrenched; and Israel's dependence on American aid, measured in absolute terms and as a percentage of gross domestic product, diminished sharply. Israel launched no aggressive wars. Instead it recognized the PLO and turned formerly occupied territory over to exclusive Palestinian control. Politicians across the Israeli spectrum either welcomed or resigned themselves to the inevitability of a Palestinian state.

In an article published ten years later, in 1998, Beinin noted the "contraction" of Israel's "military-industrial complex," the "dramatic expansion of high-technology export industries," and the triumph of a "peace and privatization" agenda. He also acknowledged that these changes "may mark an end to the specific configuration of power and culture examined here."[74] But he made no effort to reexamine that configuration himself, and no admission that he had failed to anticipate its transformation. Beinin's failure, and MERIP's failure more generally, was an ideological one: their understanding of Israel remained frozen in the late 1960s, after which they forgot nothing and learned nothing.

By the late 1990s, the writings on Israel by the aging radicals seemed hopelessly outdated. The sophisticated debates on Israeli history, politics, and society took place among Israeli scholars, whose major works regularly appeared in English. Israeli studies thus effectively escaped the weak gravitational pull of American academe, where they had never been particularly well served anyway. There could have been no more persuasive argument for the strength of Israel's own "civil society" than the fact that every possible school of interpretation flourished in its own universities (including, inevitably, the Saidian).

The Reckoning

Why had the new fief holders of Middle Eastern studies gotten it so utterly wrong? Their analyses were politically driven. In 1999, Lisa Anderson, political scientist at Columbia University and former head of its Middle East Institute, admitted as much. She frankly described an academic climate in which "being a little 'engagé' was not only permissible but desirable," even "liberating." Through political activism, office-bound scholars could transform themselves into champions of freedom in the eyes of their Arab friends: "We could utilize our knowledge and skills in political activity on behalf of, and in collaboration with, our colleagues, informants, and friends in the region."[75]

But the motive was not altogether selfless. Scholars of the Middle East, stuck with authoritarian despots for their subject matter, felt isolated from the exciting developments driving theory elsewhere in political science. The triumph of "civil society" in the Middle East would put Middle East scholars on par with their departmental colleagues who were busy studying real transformations elsewhere in the world. Anderson put it this way: "Political democratization promised to solve problems not only for Middle Eastern citizens who yearned for personal freedom and equality but for American political scientists who sought professional respectability and acceptance."[76] So not only high-minded ideals distorted academic perspectives. The pursuit of status and power within Hobbesian academe had corrupted the analytical environment by introducing a variable that had nothing to do with the real Middle East.

That variable took the form of theory. Middle East scholars, anxious to make their work acceptable to their disciplinary fellows, had squeezed their material into the reigning theoretical paradigm. In a "spirit of giddy optimism," concluded Anderson, "we students of democratization in the Middle East succumbed remarkably easily to the vain hope that reality would catch up to theory before we would be required to consider the limitations of the theory itself." Instead, the 1990s were "sobering." "Political democratization did not happen in most of the Middle East, and those of us who set out to support and study it were left in many respects normatively disappointed, politically unprepared, and scientifically isolated."[77]

The failure revealed still another core weakness of post-orientalist Middle Eastern studies in America. James Bill put it best: "The growing preoccupation with theory and method has resulted in increasing illiteracy in the fundamental understanding of Middle Eastern societies and politics." "Certain social scientists" possessed only an "elementary understanding of Middle Eastern history and culture."[78] Even worse, the mere possession of such understanding was suspect in the disciplines. Middle Eastern studies had become "a no-win situation," wrote Jerrold Green, "in which the mere recognition that cultural factors matter labels specialists as anti-scientific heretics by their more dogmatic colleagues."[79]

A deeper understanding of historical legacies and cultural factors might have prevented the "civil society" debacle; in its wake, a few practitioners concluded (ruefully) that political culture could not be omitted entirely. Hudson was one: "Cultural knowledge no doubt improves political analysis in some intangible way," he conceded.[80] But only Arab scholars could invoke it safely. When several of them did just that, an American political scientist noted that this sort of argument, "had it come from any other pens, would have been dismissed as stereotypical Orientalism."[81] This telling admission revealed much about the ethnic cleavage in Middle Eastern studies: only scholars of Middle Eastern origin could safely explore culture-based paradigms. The rest had to make do with "civil society" and its dead ends.

But in academic society, the "civil society" paradigm performed exactly as its practitioners had hoped it would. The foundation money that flooded into "civil society" and "democratization" projects generated a surfeit of conferences, seminars, and publications. Even if the "civil society" exercise made not one iota of difference to the Middle East, it made a huge difference to dozens of scholars, who turned it into grants, travel, and tenure. In 1997, Norton published a lecture lauding "The Virtue of Studying Civil Society."[82] Simply by their choice of subject, scholars rushed to proclaim their own virtue—above all, to their deans and colleagues. It worked. Academic market forces—the real driving forces behind theory—had placed a on this one narrow angle for viewing politics. Said once compl American academe was "choked with fundamentalism projects."

fact, it was choked with "civil society" projects. And America's "civil society" entrepreneurs were amply rewarded, even as "civil society" in the Middle East languished.

But having waged their campaign under the premise that the Middle East was no exception in theory, they had no persuasive analytical framework to explain why it remained an exception in practice. Within the universities, it was still possible to cover up the failure with a fog of verbiage. But the "civil society" debacle, following as it did the misjudgment of political Islam, did threaten the standing of Middle East specialists—this, at a time when the centers of American decisionmaking were writing them off anyway.

Notes

1. Yahya Sadowski, "The New Orientalism and the Democracy Debate," in *Political Islam: Essays from Middle East Report*, ed. Joel Beinin and Joe Stork (Berkeley: University of California Press, 1997), pp. 41–42 (first published 1993).

2. Elizabeth Warnock Fernea and Robert A. Fernea, *The Arab World: Personal Encounters* (Garden City, N.Y.: Anchor Press, 1985), pp. 204, 210.

3. E. Roger Owen, "State and Society in the Middle East," *Items* 44, no. 1 (March 1990), p. 10.

4. Michael C. Hudson, "Arab Integration: An Overview," in *Middle East Dilemma: The Politics and Economics of Arab Integration*, ed. Michael C. Hudson (New York: Columbia University Press, 1999), pp. 7–8.

5. Fernea and Fernea, *The Arab World*, p. 226.

6. Hisham Sharabi, *Palestine Guerrillas: Their Credibility and Effectiveness* (Washington, D.C.: Center for Strategic and International Studies, Georgetown University, 1970), p. 41.

7. Edward W. Said, *The Politics of Dispossession: The Struggle for Palestinian Self-Determination, 1969–1994* (New York: Pantheon Books, 1994), p. xv.

8. Philip S. Khoury, "Lessons from the Eastern Shore" (1998 Presidential Address), *MESA Bulletin* 33, no. 1 (Summer 1999), p. 5.

9. Said, *Politics of Dispossession*, p. 24.

10. Ibid., p. 25.

11. Michael C. Hudson, *The Precarious Republic: Political Modernization in Lebanon* (New York: Random House, 1968), pp. 330–31.

12. Michael C. Hudson, *Arab Politics: The Search for Legitimacy* (New Haven: Yale University Press, 1977), p. 30.

13. Michael C. Hudson, "State, Society, and Legitimacy: An Essay on Arab Political Prospects in the 1990s," in *The Next Arab Decade: Alternative Futures*, ed. Hisham Sharabi (Boulder: Westview Press, 1988), pp. 22, 35.

14. Ibid., p. 36.

15. Rashid I. Khalidi, "The Shape of Inter-Arab Politics in 1995," in *The Next Arab Decade*, pp. 57–58, 61.

16. Khalidi, quoted in "Can the Fragile Group of Anti-Iraq Nations Stand Up for Long?" *Associated Press*, October 14, 1990.

17. Khalidi, quoted in "Experts: U.S. Would Win War, But at Heavy Personnel Cost," Gannett News Service, January 5, 1991.

18. Khalidi, quoted in the *Toronto Star*, March 13, 1991.

19. Rashid I. Khalidi, "Letter from the President," *MESA Newsletter* 16, no. 1 (February 1994), p. 20.

20. Sharabi, remarks at a symposium of the Center for Policy Analysis on Palestine entitled "The Palestinians and the War in the Gulf," Watergate Hotel, transcript provided by Federal News Service, February 11, 1991.

21. Hudson, remarks on the *MacNeil/Lehrer NewsHour*, May 8, 1991.

22. Norton's bio can be found online at http://web.bu.edu/ir/faculty/norton.html

23. Augustus Richard Norton, review of *Political Liberalization and Democratization in the Arab World*, vol. 1, *Theoretical Perspectives*, in *American Political Science Review* 90, no. 4 (December 1996), p. 934. Here he named names, rejecting "essentialist assertions proffered by prominent anthropologists (e.g., Ernest Gellner), historians (e.g., Elie Kedourie), and a variety of polemicists to explain the absence of democracy in the Arab world." This short list was published safely after the deaths of Kedourie (1992) and Gellner (1995).

24. Augustus Richard Norton, "The Future of Civil Society in the Middle East," *Middle East Journal* 47, no. 2 (Spring 1993), p. 205.

25. Augustus Richard Norton and Robin Wright, "The Post-Peace Crisis in the Middle East," *Survival* 36, no. 4 (Winter 1994–95), pp. 7–8.

26. Augustus Richard Norton, "Introduction," in *Civil Society in the Middle East*, vol. 1, ed. Augustus Richard Norton (Leiden: Brill, 1995–96), pp. 2, 4.

27. Augustus Richard Norton, "Preface," in *Civil Society*, p. ix.

28. Norton, review of *Political Liberalization*, p. 934.

29. Augustus Richard Norton, "The New Media, Civic Pluralism, and the Slowly Retreating State," in *New Media in the Muslim World: The Emerging Public Sphere*, ed. Dale F. Eickelman and Jon W. Anderson (Bloomington: Indiana University Press, 1999), p. 27.

30. Emmanuel Sivan, "The Islamic Resurgence: Civil Society Strikes Back," *Journal of Contemporary History* 25, nos. 2–3 (May–June 1990), pp. 353–64. Even as late as 1997, Sivan repeated the "crisis" mantra: "Today, Arab regimes of all hues are undergoing a major crisis of legitimacy," he wrote. "As the state retreats, civil society advances." Emmanuel Sivan, "Constraints and Opportunities in the Arab World," *Journal of Democracy* 8, no. 2 (April 1997), pp. 103, 106.

31. Norton and Wright, "The Post-Peace Crisis," p. 18.

32. Augustus Richard Norton, "The Challenge of Inclusion in the Middle East," *Current History* 94, no. 588 (January 1995), p. 6.

33. See again Norton's bio at http://web.bu.edu/ir/faculty/norton.html

34. Michael C. Hudson, "Obstacles to Democratization in the Middle East," *Contention* 5, no. 2 (Winter 1996), pp. 81, 92, 96.

35. James A. Bill, "The Study of Middle East Politics, 1946–1996: A Stocktaking," *Middle East Journal* 50, no. 4 (Autumn 1996), pp. 501–2.

36. Arafat quoted in Alan Hart, *Arafat: A Political Biography* (Bloomington: Indiana University Press, 1989), p. 400.

37. Hudson, *Arab Politics*, p. 302.

38. Ibid., pp. 295–96.

39. Hisham Sharabi, "The Development of PLO Peace Policy," in *The Shaping of an Arab Statesman: Abd al-Hamid Sharaf and the Modern Arab World*, ed. Patrick Seale (London: Quartet, 1983), p. 162.

40. Edward W. Said, *The Question of Palestine* (New York: Times Books, 1979), p. 160.

41. Ibid., p. 165.

42. Ibid., p. 178.

43. Ibid., pp. 165–66.

44. Ibid., p. 166.

45. Ibid., p. 165.

46. Ibid., p. 215.

47. Rashid Khalidi, *Under Siege: P.L.O. Decisionmaking During the 1982 War* (New York: Columbia University Press, 1986), p. 194n18.

48. Ibid., p. 33.

49. Ibid., p. 32.

50. Jean Genet, *Prisoner of Love*, trans. Barbara Bray (London: Picador, 1989), p. 120. (The book was first published in French in 1986.)

51. Ibid., p. 227.

52. Khalidi, *Under Siege*, p. 102.

53. Ibid., p. 103. Despite this, later scholars continued to perpetuate the myth of the PNC, in order to establish that the movement had regressed from a lost idyll. "Put bluntly, Arafat was not (and could not have been) a dictator of the PLO," announced one American academic as late as 1997. "The Palestine National Council was the principal decision-making body of the PLO, and all Palestinian factions were represented in it." Glenn E. Robinson, *Building a Palestinian State: The Incomplete Revolution* (Bloomington: Indiana University Press, 1997), pp. 187–88.

54. Hart, *Arafat*, p. 550. Hart then set out to defend Arafat's high-handedness: "Collective leadership was a mechanism for indecision," Hart determined, and he suggested that "what some call Arafat's tendency to dictatorship could also be firm, true and at times really inspired leadership." Endorsements by Hudson and Khalidi appear on the back cover of the paperback edition.

55. Genet, *Prisoner of Love*, p. 373.

56. Edward W. Said, *Peace and Its Discontents: Essays on Palestine in the Middle East Peace Process* (New York: Vintage Books, 1996), p. 52.

57. Said, *The Politics of Dispossession*, p. xxxii.

58. Ibid., p. xviii.

59. Ibid., pp. 414–15.

60. Bill Ashcroft and Pal Ahluwalia, *Edward Said: The Paradox of Identity* (London: Routledge, 1999), p. 127.

61. Said, *The Politics of Dispossession*, p. xxxii.

62. It is Friedman's account, and not Said's, that is confirmed at length by Yezid Sayigh, *Armed Struggle and the Search for State: The Palestinian National Movement 1949–1993* (Oxford: Clarendon, 1997), especially chapter 19, "The 'Fakhani Republic.'"

63. Hisham Sharabi, "A Look Ahead: The Future State of Palestine," in *The Palestinians: New Directions*, ed. Michael C. Hudson (Washington, D.C.: Center for Contemporary Arab Studies, 1999), pp. 162–63.

64. William B. Quandt, "The Urge for Democracy," *Foreign Affairs* 73, no. 4 (July–August 1994), pp. 2–7.

65. Glenn E. Robinson, "Authoritarianism with a Palestinian Face," *Current History* 97, no. 615 (January 1998), p. 15.

66. Glenn E. Robinson, "The Growing Authoritarianism of the Arafat Regime," *Survival* 39, no. 2 (Summer 1997), p. 42.

67. Robinson, "Authoritarianism with a Palestinian Face," p. 13.

68. Ziad Abu-Amr, "Pluralism and the Palestinians," *Journal of Democracy* 7, no. 3 (July 1996), p. 87.

69. Ahmad S. Khalidi, "The Palestinians' First Excursion into Democracy," *Journal of Palestine Studies* 25, no. 4 (Summer 1996), pp. 21, 23.

70. Robinson, "The Growing Authoritarianism of the Arafat Regime," p. 42.

71. Fernea and Fernea, *The Arab World*, p. 33.

72. Joel Beinin, "Israel: The Political Economy of a Garrison State and Its Future," in *The Next Arab Decade*, pp. 242–43, 252–53.

73. Ibid., p. 242.

74. Joel Beinin, "Political Economy and Public Culture in a State of Constant Conflict: 50 Years of Jewish Statehood," *Jewish Social Studies* 4, no. 3 (Spring 1998), pp. 97, 134.

75. Lisa Anderson, "Politics in the Middle East: Opportunities and Limits in the Quest for Theory," in *Area Studies and Social Science: Strategies for Understanding Middle East Politics*, ed. Mark Tessler (Bloomington: Indiana University Press, 1999), p. 3.

76. Ibid., p. 2.

77. Ibid., pp. 2–3.

78. Bill, "The Study of Middle East Politics," p. 505.

79. Jerrold D. Green, "The Politics of Middle East Politics," *PS: Political Science* 27, no. 3 (September 1994), p. 517.

80. Michael C. Hudson, "The Political Culture Approach to Arab Democratization: The Case for Bringing It Back In, Carefully," in *Political Liberalization and Democratization in the Arab World*, vol. 1, *Theoretical Perspectives*, ed. Bahgat Korany, Rex Brynen, and Paul Noble (Boulder: Lynne Rienner, 1995), p. 73.

81. John Waterbury, "Democracy Without Democrats? The Potential for Political Liberalization in the Middle East," in *Democracy Without Democrats? The Renewal of Politics in the Muslim World*, ed. Ghassan Salamé (London: I. B. Tauris, 1994), pp. 30–31.

82. Augustus Richard Norton, "The Virtue of Studying Civil Society," in *The Civil Society Debate in Middle Eastern Studies*, ed. James Gelvin (Los Angeles: UCLA Center for Near Eastern Studies, 1997), pp. 5–31. This was a play on the title of an influential 1991 article by the late Edward Shils, "The Virtue of Civil Society."

5

The Beltway Barrier

No group, society, or civilization, so history allows us to postulate, will consistently support an intellectual endeavor unless it believes this effort to be serviceable either to its practical or to its existential needs—and one may do well to remind oneself that it is, in the last analysis, the existential need that determines what is to be recognized as socially useful and thus as a practical need.

—*Gustave von Grunebaum (1965)*[1]

Did Middle Eastern studies meet any existential need? In 1979, MESA's Board described academic Middle Eastern studies as "one of this country's greatest resources for understanding and learning to live with an ever more vital part of the world."[2] Twenty years later, it was difficult to say just whom this resource purported to serve, except itself. Not only had its champions made serious errors of estimation regarding some of the most central issues in Middle Eastern affairs. They simultaneously fenced themselves off from effective interaction with those Americans entrusted with meeting existential needs: the U.S. government.

Wooing Washington

The rise of antigovernment zealotry in Middle Eastern studies would have astonished the founders. For many of them, initial interest in the contemporary Middle East had been stirred by their military or civilian service during the Second World War. When the region became a war theatre, recalled one observer, "calls came from various government departments and agencies: the State Department, the War Department (G-2), Signal Corps, Naval Intelligence, the Office of Strategic Services (OSS), the Office of War Information, and the like." The war put Americans in the Middle East, and also brought about "the realization of the immense scientific deficit which had accumulated over a long period of time through the neglect of the modern Near East by the social sciences and not a few of the humanistic disciplines."[3]

After the war, private foundations worked to make good the "deficit." But the academics also subjected the government to heavy lobbying. In 1949, the Committee on Near Eastern Studies pointed enviously to the postwar decision of the British government to subsidize university programs on the Middle East.[4] In 1950, the executive secretary of the American Council of Learned Societies determined that even at the best American universities, "the academic structure is almost as West European centered as it was when Mecca was practically as far away as the moon." This could be repaired "only with the expenditure of large social capital, and that, in our political structure, means Federal Government funds." In particular, there was "no reason why there should not be government fellowships in Near Eastern studies precisely as there are government fellowships in atomic science. The one is just as important to the national security as the other."[5] But all of these pleas failed utterly. J. C. Hurewitz, then at Columbia, recalled that Washington urged the expansion of the field, but did so "without even a gesture of fiscal generosity." Congress was paralyzed by "diehard isolationists" and Senator Joseph McCarthy.[6]

For a full decade into the Cold War, academics cajoled and implored government for support—and got nowhere. Only after the Soviets launched *Sputnik* in 1957 did education lobbyists find an opening. America, they argued, had fallen behind Russia in education, including international education. Academic lobbyists joined with sympathetic congressmen and officials to propose "emergency" funding of education under the rubric of national defense. Some conservative congressmen remained doubtful. Senator Strom Thurmond, for one, opposed the bill, citing its "unbelievable remoteness from national defense considerations."[7] But the bill became law— the National Defense Education Act of 1958—and "defense education" quickly developed into another federal semi-entitlement, which carried no obligation for any specific contribution to America's defense.

Title VI of the act provided for the support of language and area studies, and the appropriation, administered by what was then called the Department of Health, Education, and Welfare, made possible the expansion of area studies centers. These functioned autonomously not only from other university departments; they also enjoyed autonomy from the government. In 1962, heads of centers called for an extension and enlargement of the act. In doing so, they praised the "statesmanlike and educationally informed way" in which Title VI was administered, allowing the universities to move forward "while preserving their own freedom of action and maintaining their own distinctive character."[8] The president of the American Council of Education was even more straightforward: "The Federal Government has provided its share of the financing of language and area centers without impairing the autonomy of the institutions receiving the funds; in short, Federal funds have been given without Federal control."[9] From its inception, Title VI was administered as a no-strings-attached benefit. Later, the "defense" designation was dropped altogether.

But the early leaders of Middle Eastern studies were also men (there were few women) of a patriotic disposition, who could be counted upon to help out. Having served their country during the Second World War, they felt no aversion to maintaining their contacts in Washington. This was not an "old boy" network, but a "new boy" network, of people who had come together for the first time in the defining experience of their generation. Despite widely different social and ethnic origins, they shared camaraderie and an implicit trust, and a worldview shaped by the recent conflict. In these years, as Bernard Lewis later put it, "the choices before us still retained something of the clarity, even the starkness, which they had kept through the war years and which they have subsequently lost."[10] Something of the ambiance is conveyed by Hurewitz's account of how he gained access to classified and nonclassified intelligence material for his book *Middle East Politics: The Military Dimension* (1969). A telephone call to an old OSS acquaintance; a serendipitous coincidence of interests; a security clearance and contract; and publication of the results after a speedy review—it was all fairly easygoing.[11]

Certainly government expected to reap benefits in the form of enhanced understanding, but it was believed that these would accumulate slowly, through a generalized diffusion of knowledge. Universities could do what they always did, but with far greater resources. And in the 1960s, money was so easy that only new centers competed for funds; centers, once funded, enjoyed automatic renewal of their grants.

The Great Divide

The gap between Washington and academe began to open during the years of radical politicization of the campus in the mid-1960s. The U.S. Army–sponsored Project Camelot, meant to mobilize area studies for in-country counterinsurgency research, evoked a strong backlash in academe, the Department of State, and Congress. (Project Camelot began its operations in Chile. But according to its plan, the project would have eventually included Army-sponsored social science research in Iran, Egypt, and Turkey.) The Department of Defense had overreached.

But the episode became a narrow prism through which academics continued to view relations with government. Even when the circumstances that produced Project Camelot disappeared, many academics instinctively regarded any government initiative as a potential Project Camelot, and reacted accordingly. As it turned out, the idea of a pervasive Department of Defense "penetration" of academe was a myth; as a 1973 survey of area specialists revealed, "the radical caucuses' concern about the dread impact of military support for academic area research seems numerically to be unjustified."[12] But suspicions in academe fed upon themselves, and the divide widened.

By the time Richard Nixon entered the White House in 1969, area studies no longer rested on a Washington consensus, and Nixon's administration immediately set out to eliminate support for all area studies centers, including those devoted to the Middle East. In his 1970 budget message, Nixon listed the National Defense Education Act as one of the "less productive and outmoded programs." In the words of MESA's president at the time, this "led to one of the greatest lobbying efforts ever conducted by educators in this county," involving university presidents, center directors, and area studies associations.[13] Friends in Congress managed to ward off the attack, but not before the administration succeeded in halving the budget (funding of Middle East centers was halved almost exactly). Funds were restored in 1972, but in 1973, the Department of Education halved the number of area studies centers and cut the number of Middle East centers from twelve to seven.[14] In 1974, the administration zero-budgeted Title VI and again proposed to eliminate the program. Henry Kissinger and Senator Daniel Patrick Moynihan intervened with Nixon, but it was Congress that saved the day. In the new climate, the government required that all center grants be awarded exclusively through a competition, and that 15 percent of center funding be used for "outreach" beyond the campus.[15]

By the time Edward Said sat down to write *Orientalism* in 1975, the leaders of Middle Eastern studies knew something he did not know or preferred to ignore: the days of relaxed reliance on Washington were over. Even before the Middle Eastern studies "establishment" came under assault from the left, it found itself under attack by the right, which identified no real benefit from university-based programs and centers.

This view also percolated through the bureaucracy. In 1979, a RAND report on area studies noted that government analysts displayed an "attitude of condescension or flat dismissal toward academics, who 'don't really know what is going on' or—as in the common State Department view—are engaged in research that is not directly relevant to policymaking."[16] In 1981, a RAND report on Title VI singled out Middle East scholars for their lack of communication with policymakers: "We found in talking with faculty at area centers that their own training often makes it difficult for them to translate scholarly research into an applied format useful to policymakers. This is particularly true for humanities faculty who presently dominate some of the largest Middle Eastern centers."[17]

Fortunately for the Middle East centers, they were part of the wider framework of Title VI, which was on its way to becoming a secure semi-entitlement, backed up by the full weight of the higher education lobby. In the first years of Ronald Reagan's presidency, one last attempt was made to zero-budget Title VI. The academics rushed to persuade Secretary of Defense Caspar Weinberger to intervene on their behalf, which he did, and the appropriation was saved once again at the eleventh hour.[18] Since that time, Title VI funding has remained constant in some years and has increased in others.

But the frustration in Washington also remained constant, and in some years increased. This was especially the case in the 1980s and 1990s, when various government agencies tried to derive some benefit, however marginal, from the existence of so many federally subsidized centers, programs, scholars, and students devoted to the Middle East. Their efforts were often clumsy, and their authors demonstrated an imperfect grasp of the workings of academe. More importantly, government seemed unaware of the revolution that had taken place in Middle Eastern studies. These had come to be dominated by the American generation formed by the Vietnam war, and an Arab generation formed by the 1967 Arab-Israeli war and the Palestinian awakening. Many of the insurgents, in their bid for academic power, had denounced established scholars for their alleged complicity with the American government. Once in power, they proceeded to erect high ramparts between the field and Washington, and to patrol them with a zealotry that would lead many officials to write off academe altogether.

Rules of Excommunication

The earliest example of a coordinated campaign against government-sponsored research followed upon the creation, in 1981, of the Defense Academic Research Support Program (DARSP). This program, established under the Defense Intelligence Agency (DIA) and later placed under the Defense Intelligence College, invited "unclassified, publishable research studies using only open source material," which would "supplement analyses and policy deliberations within the Defense Department."[19] The program shifted its focus to the Middle East in 1983, and eventually settled upon researching sources of domestic instability, a perennial subject of academic and government interest. Title VI center directors received a circular about the new program and were asked to bring it to the attention of faculty.

The combination of "defense," "intelligence," and "agency" had an immediate effect: MESA's ethics committee launched a campaign to discredit the initiative and deter scholars from responding to it. The very fact that an intelligence agency was known to solicit research would "pose hazards in the conduct of field research" by all scholars. The program, "even if conducted openly and using only unrestricted materials, is liable to have negative consequences for foreign research opportunities, even if such research is conducted entirely within this country."[20] The ethics experts thus determined that any American scholar engaged in government-sponsored research, even one doing so from the comfort of his office and relying on books, articles, and newspapers, still constituted a dire threat to his colleagues and the entire field.

As the MESA committee report put it, the DIA was surprised by the "intensity of objections."[21] It must have been: a government agency could be excused for not discerning an ethical problem. What could be unethical about openly declared research assistance, voluntarily rendered to one's own government, done at home and on the basis of sources available to anyone, and destined for publication? In fact, MESA's position was political, not ethical. Its politics were leftovers from the years of radical alienation from

American policy and from the very concepts of defense and intelligence. In November 1985, MESA passed its final verdict, calling upon "university-based international studies programs to refrain from responding to requests for research contract proposals" from DARSP, and asking MESA members "to reflect carefully upon their responsibilities to the academic profession prior to seeking or accepting funding from intelligence sources."[22] In the end, only a few souls braved this implicit threat of excommunication.[23] As one keen observer of the culture of area studies put it, "scholars too closely iden- tified with [the Department of Defense] or intelligence affairs are viewed by some of their American colleagues as volunteering for terminal leprosy."[24] As the DARSP affair first showed, such colleagues now set the tone for all of Middle Eastern studies.

A second episode in 1985 caused an even greater storm. Nadav Safran, director of Harvard's Center for Middle Eastern Studies, accepted a CIA offer to fund a conference on Islam and politics—this, after three founda- tions turned down his proposal. Safran decided not to inform the invitees of the source of funding, fearing they might cancel their participation. When Harvard's student newspaper revealed the CIA funding five days before the conference, a scandal erupted.

Safran did violate an ethical principle by not informing all the partici- pants of the funding source. Had the CIA involvement become known only later, it could have exposed the Middle Eastern participants to accusations of connivance with a foreign intelligence agency. No one genuinely familiar with the mindset of Islamic extremism in the 1980s would have exposed his Middle Eastern guests to such a risk. Safran was also in clear violation of MESA's standards: in 1982, MESA had called on "organizations and institu- tions in Middle East Studies to make regular disclosure of the sources of funding for their programs, conferences, and activities as they are announced and take place, and calls on its members to urge such disclosure."[25] Finally, Safran seemed oblivious to the fact that Harvard was and remains the most scrutinized of all American universities, always held to a more exacting standard.

But MESA's leaders again protested too much, by claiming that Safran had endangered the image of American scholarship, or even endangered American scholars. "News of the relationship between some Middle East schol- ars and the intelligence agencies has a devastating effect upon the image of our field in Middle Eastern countries," preached Kemal Karpat, MESA's presi- dent, at the next annual conference. "There is now the frightening prospect that any scholar, however disinterested and honest, working in the Middle East may be regarded by some local extremist group as an intelligence agent and may be kidnapped or killed. . . . The greed and ambition of one or two of our colleagues thus may injure us all and destroy our chosen field of research."[26]

In its imputation of motives (as though "greed and ambition" exhausted the reasons for rendering service to one's government), the address constituted an exercise in demagoguery. But the argument itself was absurd, if only because, as William Quandt rightly pointed out, "Americans working in the Middle East have always been suspected of working for the CIA. Middle Easterners believe that as an article of faith."[27]

This impression was only fortified by other American academics, who used charges of espionage to discredit their own academic rivals. In 1974, the Northwestern University political scientist Ibrahim Abu-Lughod published an article in Arabic in a leading Beirut journal, claiming that the Middle East centers at Princeton, Chicago, Harvard, and UCLA were "Zionist instruments and bases for Israeli-American espionage."[28] Before the Safran affair, Edward Said's *Covering Islam* had made its way into the hands of Islamic Jihad in Lebanon. In its authoritative pages, the real kidnappers could read that in America, all Middle East scholars were "affiliated to the mechanism by which national policy is set. This is not a matter of choice for the individual scholar."[29] Safran's error created no danger to American scholars that Said's (and Abu-Lughod's) libels had not created already. Yet Said was canonized for fanning the suspicions of "extremists," whereas Safran was censured for it. The difference, of course, had to do with politics.

As it happened, Safran had conducted himself like most other center directors, who routinely obscured information about funding. "My guess is that most people in our field, aside from those who run centers, have little idea where money in the field comes from," said Nikki Keddie in her MESA presidential address only four years earlier. "They might like to know, but an unwarranted atmosphere of secrecy makes asking questions seem like prying."[30]

The secrecy arose in the 1970s, when some Arab governments and Iran made large grants to American universities and Middle East programs. When a scandal broke in 1979 regarding one such program in California, the California State Senate passed a resolution urging full disclosure of terms and conditions of such grants. MESA, in contrast, did not pass such a resolution. Instead, its Board of Directors issued a blanket assurance that "the scholars and administrators engaged in university programs in Middle East studies are capable of administering these funds in a professionally responsible fashion."[31] Three more years elapsed before MESA passed its own disclosure resolution. (Today, disclosure is the law, as provided by the University Disclosure Act of 1986, which compels the disclosure of any large foreign grant to an institution that receives federal support.)[32] In fact, the prevailing standards of disclosure in Middle Eastern studies were inconsistent, selective, and political.

Needless to say, the post-orientalists, after their seizure of academic power, did not establish a notably higher standard of disclosure than their predecessors—even at Harvard. Roger Owen, seated in the very same director's chair at the Center for Middle Eastern Studies, inaugurated a new "Contemporary Arab Studies Program" in 1995. The program's brochure offered this informative statement about the source of its money: "The Program is being initiated by generous new funding not currently available to the university."[33] In practical terms, the only kind of research funding that the academics insisted be disclosed in full and in public came from Washington. And by any calculation, accepting such funding, in the inquisitorial atmosphere of Middle Eastern studies, was more trouble than it was worth.

An Abuse of Trust

There was, however, an exception. The truly pure at heart, those whose disdain for Washington was so total as to banish any thought of corruption, could allow themselves to solicit government. This happened in the aftermath of the Gulf War, when the new establishment decided to take advantage of increased public interest and lobby for a new public subsidy.

The appeal to Washington was full of irony. Most academics had opposed American policy in the lead-up to the war, and had disparaged American performance right through its end. The keenest military observer of Middle Eastern studies expressed the general view that the academics had misread the war and its aftermath, but refused to "go back to the basics and figure out why." Until they did, their "diminished reputation [would] not improve."[34] Still, the Gulf War gave unprecedented public exposure to academics, and the new mandarins of Middle Eastern studies understood that if Washington's purse were ever to open again, this would be the moment. Their objective was to secure a clear-cut semi-entitlement, essentially expanding the Title VI subsidy they had enjoyed for more than thirty years.

In an irony on top of irony, the Social Science Research Council led the campaign. This venerable New York institution, the self-proclaimed presidium of area studies, always had a sharp nose for the latest trend. In the 1980s, it turned over the prestigious Joint Committee on the Near and Middle East to the post-orientalists, to do with as they pleased. Under its new guard, the SSRC committee dispensed graduate and faculty fellowships and convened meetings (often in exotic places) that inevitably revolved around the latest academic fad.[35] The sponsored work became progressively more arcane, and ever more remote from anything that might interest anyone beneath the most rarified strata of academe.

This included anyone responsible for thinking about American policy. In looking over SSRC grants for the Middle East, Judith Tucker, one of the new guard, reported happily in 1985 that funded research bore "less of the imprint of stringent policy demands" than in the past. "Topics which reflect a new breadth of interest, such as the history of blindness and the blind in medieval Islam or the political culture of Egyptian workers, also have entered the lists." Her only regret was that SSRC-sponsored research was "not entirely free of the test of relevance to policy concerns."[36] For this author— and for the committee members as well—the true measure of the SSRC's final liberation would be its total and absolute irrelevance to policy.

Yet the SSRC still enjoyed an aura of prestige in Washington, where the Gulf War created what an SSRC program officer called "an opportunity to mobilize Congressional support for expanded federal funding for scholarly research on the Middle East." While the Gulf guns were still smoking—in March 1991—the SSRC's Joint Committee on the Near and Middle East solemnly "agreed to pursue this opportunity, and to initiate efforts to create a federal program of research and training on the region." Senator Richard Lugar and the Senate Foreign Relations Committee took up the idea, and the Senate even accepted the SSRC's draft legislation. It constituted a wish list of Middle Eastern studies: graduate training, at home and abroad; advanced research fellowships and grant support; conferences and publications; and much more. And while the program would come under the general auspices of the Department of State, the bureaucrats would not pass out the money. This would be done by "national organizations with an interest and expertise in conducting research and training concerning the countries of the Near and Middle East." They would run the competitions, based on peer review. The program officer at the SSRC, in reporting to MESA, celebrated the "absence of restrictions" in the act imposed on scholars; it was "entirely unrestricted" as to the topics that could be funded.[37] Another great entitlement seemed to have been bagged—and the SSRC seemed certain to administer it.

In October 1992, Congress finally appropriated funds for the program. True, the idea had been trimmed during its passage through the bureaucratic mill. Congress transferred administration of the program from the Department of State to the U.S. Information Agency, which meant it could only fund Americans abroad. There would be no fellowships and grants to hand out at home. And, given the emphasis on activity abroad, the SSRC would administer only part of the funds. Overseas research institutes, such as the American Research Center in Egypt, would receive a substantial share. Special preference would be given to the neglected disciplines of sociology and economics. In the SSRC, one could detect a sense of disappointment with these "more targeted programmatic priorities."[38] This would not be Title VI all over again. Yet it did represent a substantial windfall for the Middle Eastern studies brigade. In 1998, for example, the SSRC alone distributed thirty-two grants under the program, known as NMERTP (Near and Middle East Research and Training Program).[39]

Five years after the inauguration of NMERTP, its administrators at the U.S. Information Agency announced that the program—"designed to meet the national security needs of the United States"—had "provided a broad and diverse range of students and scholars with financial assistance," registering "a steady improvement in the quality of individual grantees."[40] To judge from the SSRC's grants, none of this was true. The fellowships committee resembled a politburo of the like-minded—most of them adherents of the (neo-Marxist) political economy school—and almost none of the grant topics had any possible relevance to the national security of the United States. Indeed, they precisely reflected the long-term trend within the SSRC *away* from such subjects.

Through the mediation of post-orientalist peer review, NMERTP eventually revealed itself as something very different from a program designed to address national security needs, however obliquely. To the contrary, it looked like a successful academic sting operation on Congress. Flush with taxpayers' money, dozens of scholars rushed off to the Middle East to conduct ever-more-obscure research on "masculinities in Egypt," "perceptions of the deaf in Islamic society," or "the dance of the Nubians."[41] This sort of research might have been funded legitimately out of money provided by the National Endowment for the Humanities (which, in earlier years, did support SSRC fellowships). But to fund it out of NMERTP was an abuse, even if the program rules did not explicitly restrict research topics.

Not surprisingly, support for the program began to evaporate, and so did the appropriation. When the Department of State absorbed the U.S. Information Agency in 1999, it phased out NMERTP. After the SSRC abolished all the area studies committees in 1996, NMERTP had been the only crutch of Middle Eastern studies at the council. Once it disappeared, so too did the council's last specifically Middle Eastern grant program.

There was no other way to put it: the new guild masters had killed the golden goose. Circumstances had granted them a rare chance to expand federal support for Middle Eastern studies—the first such opportunity in more than thirty years, and one that would never have come about "were it not for Iraq's invasion of Kuwait, the Gulf War, and the postwar Arab-Israeli diplomatic process."[42] Had there been visionary leaders in the field, a minimal understanding of Washington's ways, and a willingness to promote some genuine diversity, NMERTP could have become as steady a funding source as Title VI. Instead, the program was squandered on rewards for the faithful and produced nothing that answered public needs. Above all, it epitomized the total failure of the new mandarins to assume mature responsibility for the welfare of their field.

A Battle Lost

This alone should have sufficed to dissuade anyone in Washington of the trustworthiness of academic Middle Eastern studies. But it was compounded by MESA's conduct over another government initiative.

Senator David Boren chaired the Senate Select Committee on Intelligence during the collapse of the Soviet Union and the Gulf War. As a witness to numerous intelligence lapses, he came to believe that American national security would be served by sending more students to study abroad and encouraging more students to take up the study of a world region in their own universities. The government would subsidize the studies of these students in return for a modest service obligation. Perhaps some of them would stay on in government service. In 1991, Boren took advantage of a post–Cold War surplus in the intelligence budget to push through the National Security Education Act, designed to promote precisely this agenda.

For bureaucratic and political reasons, the program came to rest in the Department of Defense. But it would dispense the scholarships, on the basis of merit, as re-grants through contracted academic institutions. Ultimate responsibility for the program would rest with the National Security Education Board, consisting of federal officials representing the worlds of intelligence, defense, diplomacy, and commerce, as well as presidential appointees subject to Senate confirmation. The plan also involved a great deal of money: the proceeds of a projected $150 million national trust fund.

Not surprisingly, the National Security Education Program (NSEP) immediately became a rallying point for academic radicals of every stripe. They again conjured up the image of intelligence agencies sending tentacles into the academy, and the mainstream area studies organizations mobilized to wrest the program from the Department of Defense—an impossible outcome, given the legislative origins of the program. The SSRC, in particular, began to wrangle with Boren's people, proposing modifications and supposed improvements, the effect of which would have been to turn the program into one more semi-entitlement.[43]

MESA's resolutions during the controversy simply rehashed the old themes of every past controversy. In 1992, its Board of Directors "deplore[d] the location of responsibility [for the program] in the U.S. defense and intelligence community." This would "create dangers for students and scholars by fostering the perception of involvement in military or intelligence activities." MESA called on Boren to "ensure that the priorities, criteria, and funding goals of the program are developed from within the academic community," and that the program be guided by "university-based foreign area studies experts who have a wide-ranging and long-term view of national needs." (MESA meant its own leaders.) MESA ended by urging members and their institutions "not to seek or accept program or research funding" until the academics got their way.[44] In short, the academics wanted to reenact the miracle of Title VI and would accept nothing less.

What the academics failed to fathom was that Congress did not intend to create another Title VI. True, Boren repeatedly described his proposal as "the first major national security education initiative undertaken in this country since the passage of the National Defense Education Act [in 1958]."[45] But it was precisely because Title VI did *not* meet national security needs that Congress had agreed to support an entirely new program. Following the Cold War and the Gulf War, Congress really meant it: the U.S. government needed cadres educated in international affairs. Congress was prepared to contract their education to the universities, but it had no intention of establishing another semi-entitlement for the tenured class and their enrolled acolytes.

Nevertheless, the NSEP's planners in the Department of Defense went to great lengths to secure the good will of academics in the major centers. They appointed a director with academic credentials; they moved the program physically out of the Pentagon; and they progressively watered down the service requirement so that it could be met almost anywhere in government, in parts of the private sector, and even in education. But they could not meet the real requirement of the academics, which was to provide them with an obligation-free entitlement to do what they were doing anyway. In 1994, as the program got underway, the NSEP invited MESA to nominate reviewers for proposals and applications for institutional grants. MESA pointedly declined.[46] Later, a former MESA president, John Voll, did agree to serve on the program's academic Advisory Group.

The NSEP subsequently became a bone of contention within Congress. Democrats stoked the fantasies of the academics by proposing to move the entire program to the Department of Education for incorporation into Title VI.[47] Republicans wanted to cut the program altogether, or at least guarantee that all fellowship holders meet their service obligation in the Department of Defense or intelligence agencies (an idea opposed by the Department and the agencies themselves). "Congress intends to use the program to recruit young people into the intelligence services," warned MESA's president, Ann Mosley Lesch, "by offering the tempting bait of fellowships at a time when scholarship funds are limited."[48] In 1997, a compromise forged by Senator Paul Simon salvaged the program and preserved most of its original service options, although the NSEP lost half of its planned endowment.

NSEP's administrators learned their lesson: Congress, not MESA presidents, would determine whether the program lived or died. To protect it, they dropped their efforts to appease the unappeasable elites of area studies. In the process, the NSEP became a program of fellowships and institutional support for lesser universities which did not enjoy the largesse of Title VI. And, behold, it began to generate new opportunities for language study, foreign travel, and area learning for thousands of students, many of them from practical disciplines outside the humanities and social sciences. The service requirement assured that many of these graduates would make their way permanently into government, where they would have a real influence on American policy—an influence MESA seemed intent upon denying itself. The lords of area studies reassured themselves that the NSEP had "become marginal, misguided, and essentially inconsequential."[49] In fact, its impact in Washington, over the longer term, promised to be central, focused, and very consequential.

By the end of the 1990s, criticism of the NSEP began to fade after it became clear that the program had not coerced or seduced anyone. The international education lobby even began asking for an increase in the NSEP's budget. The program, in the words of a headline in the *Chronicle of Higher Education,* had been "a sheep in wolf's clothing."[50] But no retractions were issued by MESA, which in its hysteria had nearly deprived countless students of the opportunity to study the Middle East at home and abroad. Even as late as 2000, MESA past-president Philip Khoury wrote that "MESA believes students who take NSEP funds are at risk owing to their association with an organization that has direct connections to the United States intelligence community."[51]

No doubt there were many in MESA who, looking back on the controversies of the 1980s and 1990s, took pride in their spirited defense of academic freedom against the military-intelligence nexus. But from the outside, they looked like a band of graying radicals and conspiracy theorists, tilting at windmills. They had fought repeated attempts to infuse government funds into Middle Eastern studies because Washington politics required their inclusion in "defense" packages. (Did they not remember that even Title VI, the greatest of all unencumbered semi-entitlements, had been born under a "defense" star?) When they did land one new subsidy, NMERTP, they promptly lost it by promoting self-indulgent research.

The vocal expressions of distrust for the agencies of a democratic government also guaranteed that academic criticisms of policy would be taken with a shaker of salt. Ironically, this became a cause of academic complaint. Rashid Khalidi, as president of MESA, lamented "the degree to which expertise on the Middle East is simply ignored by governments and, to a lesser degree, the media and other institutions of civil society."[52] In 1998, Jerrold Green, a RAND analyst and former director of the Middle East center at the University of Arizona, wrote of the "persistent irrelevance [of Middle East scholars] in the formulation of U.S. Middle East policy. Some Middle East experts feel that they hold the keys to a successful U.S. role in the region. Unfortunately for them, the policy community seems to disagree."[53] They disagreed not only because the academic experts got things wrong, but because the new Middle East studies establishment persisted in questioning the bona fides of just about every department and agency that tried to build a bridge to them.

In 1998, Anthony Cordesman, national security analyst at the Center for Strategic and International Studies in Washington, told a congressional committee that Middle East specialists were useless in the effort to define and advance American interests:

> Unfortunately, many U.S. Middle East experts are anything but an asset in this battle. They provide a chorus of almost ritual criticism of any U.S. military role in the region, and any use of force. . . . [They] generally do a far better job of speaking for the country or countries they study than for the U.S. While this is true of most regional experts in all regions, it is one of the

ironies of Middle East studies that U.S. Middle East experts do a far better job of reaching out to the region than they do to U.S. policy makers.[54]

This last statement neatly summarized Washington's dismissive attitude toward the academic study of the Middle East. In the centers of policy, defense, and intelligence, consensus held that little could be learned from academics—not because they knew nothing, but because they deliberately withheld their knowledge from government, or organized it on the basis of arcane priorities or conflicting loyalties.

A Convenient Ally

There was, however, one instance in which Middle Eastern studies averted their gaze when government did use a scholar for its own ends. That scholar was John Esposito.

In the 1990s, Esposito, champion of Islamism as a movement of democratic reform, found enthusiastic allies in the Department of State. These officials desired indirect lines of communication to Islamists who seemed to be within striking distance of power. This kind of contact was extremely difficult to undertake in the Middle East, where friendly regimes saw any American overture to their Islamist opponents as betrayal. As early as 1985, Esposito went before a congressional committee to urge that these American diplomats and analysts be allowed "increased contacts and dialogue with Islamic leaders."[55] Esposito, who had plenty of such contacts, later became a "consultant to the Department of State and multinational corporations."[56] His vita listed him as a "foreign affairs analyst" for the Near East and South Asia branch of the Bureau of Intelligence and Research, Department of State, and as a consultant to Exxon, Texaco, Aramco, and United Technologies.[57]

Government advocates of contacts with Islamists eagerly welcomed Esposito's arrival at Georgetown. Robert H. Pelletreau, then head of Near Eastern affairs at the Department of State, spoke at the inauguration of Esposito's Center for Muslim-Christian Understanding, which he later praised as a meeting place from which "modernizing interpretations of Islam will begin to emerge."[58] The new U.S. Institute of Peace (USIP), closely attuned to the priorities of the Department of State, was also forthcoming. In 1992, Esposito and Voll received from the American taxpayer, through USIP, $58,960 for a project on Islamism and democracy.[59] The institute also co-sponsored the first international conference of the new Center for Muslim-Christian Understanding in 1994.[60] Esposito provided one of government's niche needs—a small insurance policy covering Islamists—and the premiums followed. "Anything said about Islam by a professional scholar is within the sphere of influence of corporations and the government," Edward Said had written. If this were true of anyone, it was certainly true, *prima facie*, of Esposito.

Yet when it came to Esposito, the Saidians suddenly suspended their critical faculties. There was good reason. Said himself approved of the "sensible and cogently argued book *The Islamic Threat*,"[61] where Esposito carried forward the Saidian project against orientalism's latest mutations. ("New forms of orientalism flourish today," warned Esposito, complaining against "stereotypes" in academia, government, the media, publishing houses, journals, and consulting firms.)[62] Esposito echoed Said; Said then echoed Esposito in an essay entitled "The Phony Islamic Threat," published by the *New York Times Magazine*.[63] Both declared the "Islamic threat" a concoction of the media, the experts, and the bureaucrats, who were prejudiced against Muslims and eager to substitute Islam for the Soviet Union as the new evil empire.

No wonder, then, that the Saidian watchdogs did not protest against Esposito's "complicity" with government and the corporations. No wonder, then, that the MESA ethics committee forgot to warn against the damage Esposito's intelligence and corporate connections might do to the reputation of all scholars in the field. For on the political issues of importance to the new masters of Middle Eastern studies, Esposito was perfectly aligned. He was the most visible beneficiary of the blatant double standard that now prevailed in Middle Eastern studies. Those who dissented from prevailing orthodoxies were banned from dealing with their government. Those who upheld the dogma received limited licenses to do just that.

Esposito did deserve credit for his ability to communicate with Washington. While other academics retreated to their towers, Esposito artfully presented his ideas in the public arena. These ideas did not prevail, because they were conceived in error. But Esposito provided a model of entrepreneurship, engagement, and relevance. It was a model, however, that only underlined the inconsistency of the standards that organized Middle Eastern studies purported to uphold.

Second Thoughts

By the mid-1990s, some leaders of the guild began to appreciate the damage they had done to the field by alienating themselves from policymakers. Rashid Khalidi was the first to realize the obvious: if academics could not make persuasive cases in Washington, this would undermine their standing on campus. "If we have no clout in terms of policy-making," he asked in 1994, "and can't get our message across on that level, then how can we expect the state legislators, university trustees, potential funders, foundation officials and university administrators on whom our fate depends to listen to us?"[64] "If we fail to get out of our rut," Khalidi warned an assembled MESA that year, "our marginalization will spread beyond the current level of policy and public discourse, and will extend into our own cherished preserve of academia."[65] Philip Khoury, a savvy administrator raised inside the Beltway, reached a similar conclusion in 1998:

We must accept a higher degree of accountability than we have been used to and turn this accountability to our advantage by communicating effectively with the American public and the federal government about what we do and why it is important. We must leverage our position by utilizing, more than we have, traditional mechanisms of outreach such as writing opinion editorials and essays in national and local newspapers and magazines and lobbying our elected representatives and federal agencies.[66]

How did it come to pass that two presidents of MESA, both disciples of Edward Said, should be calling upon their colleagues—most of them disciples of Said—to influence Washington policymaking, communicate effectively with the federal government, and lobby federal agencies? Said's admirers, who were now the lords of Middle Eastern studies (and MESA), had begun to realize that they had undermined the crucial foundations of external support for Middle Eastern studies. The federal subsidy for Middle Eastern studies came to several millions of taxpayer dollars annually. These subsidies paid for instructorships, student fellowships, outreach programs, and library resources. The designation of a center as a National Resource Center, in a nationwide competition, impressed provosts and deans and made it easier to attract funding from foundations. And the existence of these centers buttressed the standing of the field as a whole, creating openings at other institutions. To keep the funds flowing, both Khalidi and Khoury now believed that the field had to impress itself on Washington.

But by the time they realized this, Middle Eastern studies had lost the trust of the general public. Even worse, they were losing credibility within the academy itself.

Notes

1. Gustave E. von Grunebaum, "Specialization," in *Arabic and Islamic Studies in Honor of Hamilton A. R. Gibb*, ed. George Makdisi (Cambridge: Harvard University Press, 1965), p. 285.

2. Resolution by the Board of Directors, *MESA Newsletter* 2, no. 1 (Spring 1980), p. 2.

3. E. A. Speiser, "Near Eastern Studies in America, 1939–45," *Archiv Orientální* (Prague) 16, nos. 1–2 (December 1947), p. 87.

4. Committee on Near Eastern Studies, *A Program for Near Eastern Studies in the United States* (Washington, D.C.: American Council of Learned Societies, 1949), p. 12.

5. Mortimer Graves, "A Cultural Relations Policy in the Near East," in *The Near East and the Great Powers*, ed. Richard N. Frye (Cambridge: Harvard University Press, 1951), pp. 76–77. The Rockefeller Foundation had sent Graves, the area studies promoter of the American Council of Learned Societies, on an "extended tour" of the Middle East in 1948 and 1949, "in order to gain first-hand information on local conditions and the possibilities for American educational cooperation." Committee on Near Eastern Studies, *A Program for Near Eastern Studies*, p. 1.

6. J. C. Hurewitz, "The Education of J. C. Hurewitz," in *Paths to the Middle East: Ten Scholars Look Back*, ed. Thomas Naff (Albany: State University of New York Press, 1993), p. 96.

7. Quoted by Barbara Barksdale Clowse in *Brainpower for the Cold War: The Sputnik Crisis and the National Defense Education Act of 1958* (Westport, Conn.: Greenwood Press, 1981), p. 126.

8. Statement of 53 University Foreign Language and Area Center Directors on Title VI of the National Defense Education Act, October 14, 1962, in Donald L. Bigelow and Lyman H. Legters, *NDEA Language and Area Centers: A Report on the First 5 Years* (Washington, D.C.: U.S. Department of Health, Education, and Welfare, 1964), p. 79. The signatories included Gustave von Grunebaum of UCLA, Majid Khadduri of Johns Hopkins, T. Cuyler Young of Princeton, and Aziz Atiya of Utah—all of them heads of the original group of Title VI Middle East centers.

9. Logan Wilson, quoted in ibid., p. 3. A Council report indicated that Title VI had been administered "without the slightest government interference," "recognizing the right of a center to self-determination." Joseph Axelrod and Donald N. Bigelow, *Resources for Language and Area Studies: A Report on an Inventory of the Language and Area Centers Supported by the National Defense Education Act of 1958* (Washington, D.C.: American Council on Education, 1962), pp. 2–3.

10. Bernard Lewis, "Modern Turkey Revisited," *Humanities* 11, no. 3 (May–June 1990), p. 12.

11. Hurewitz, "The Education of J. C. Hurewitz," pp. 93–94.

12. Only 2.6 percent of specialists reported ever receiving research support from the Department of Defense or the Office of Naval Research. Richard D. Lambert, *Language and Area Studies Review* (Philadelphia: American Academy of Political and Social Science, October 1973), p. 51.

13. William M. Brinner, "1970 Presidential Address," *MESA Bulletin* 5, no. 1 (February 1, 1971), p. 3.

14. Deborah Shapley, "Middle East Studies: Funding Wilts as Arab-U.S. Friendship Flowers," *Science* 185 (July 5, 1974), pp. 42–44.

15. On the implementation of "outreach," see Kathleen Manning, *Outreach Educational Activities of Title VI National Resource Centers in International Studies: A Study Report with Recommendations* (Albany: Center for International Programs and Comparative Studies, State University of New York, 1983).

16. Sue E. Berryman, Paul E. Langer, John Pincus, and Richard H. Solomon, *Foreign Language and International Studies Specialists: The Marketplace and National Policy* (Santa Monica: RAND, September 1979), p. 98.

17. Lorraine M. McDonnell, Sue E. Berryman, and Douglas Scott, *Federal Support for International Studies: The Role of NDEA Title VI* (Santa Monica: RAND, May 1981), p. 30.

18. Richard D. Lambert, "History and Future of HEA Title VI," *Position Papers on Foreign Language Policy* (Washington, D.C.: National Foreign Language Center, October 1991), p. 3; Gilbert W. Merkx, "Plus ça Change: Challenges to Graduate Education under HEA Title VI," in *International Education in the New Global Era: Proceedings of a National Policy Conference on the Higher Education Act, Title VI, and Fulbright-Hays Programs*, ed. John N. Hawkins et al. (Los Angeles: International Studies and Overseas Program, University of California, Los Angeles, 1998), p. 77.

19. DIA circular, quoted in "A Report to the MESA Membership from the Ethics Committee, November 1984," *MESA Newsletter* 7, no. 1 (Winter 1985), p. 8.

20. Ibid., pp. 8–9. The committee members were Dale Eickelman and Marilyn Waldman.

21. Ibid., p. 8.

22. Text of resolution, *MESA Bulletin* 20, no. 1 (July 1986), pp. 4–5.

23. The most notable Middle Eastern study to emerge from the project dealt with Jewish extremism in Israel: Ian S. Lustick, *For the Land and the Lord: Jewish Fundamentalism in Israel* (New York: Council on Foreign Relations, 1988). Lustick: "This book originated in a research paper written under contract for the Defense Academic Research Support Program of the United States Department of Defense."

24. Richard D. Lambert, "DoD, Social Science, and International Studies," *Annals of the American Academy of Political and Social Science* 502 (March 1989), pp. 104–5.

25. *MESA Bulletin* 17, no. 1 (July 1983), p. 119.

26. Kemal Karpat, "Remarks on MESA and the Nation and Nationality in the Middle East" (1985 Presidential Address), *MESA Bulletin* 20, no. 1 (July 1986), p. 4.

27. William Quandt quoted in Robert I. Friedman, "Harvard, the C.I.A. and the Middle East," *Present Tense* 13, no. 3 (Spring 1986), p. 8.

28. Ibrahim Abu-Lughod, "Al-Saytara al-Sahyuniyya 'ala al-dirasat al-'arabiyya fi Amrika" (Zionist control over Arab studies in America), *Al-Adab* 12, no. 6 (June 1974), p. 6.

29. Edward W. Said, *Covering Islam* (New York: Pantheon Books, 1981), pp. 19, 158.

30. Nikki R. Keddie, "Money and Ethics in Middle East Studies" (1981 Presidential Address), *MESA Bulletin* 16, no. 1 (July 1982), pp. 6–7.

31. "Resolution by the Board of Directors," *MESA Newsletter* 2, no. 1 (Spring 1980), p. 2.

32. This amendment to the Higher Education Act requires academic institutions enjoying federal support to inform the Department of Education of any foreign grant or contract worth $250,000 or more.

33. Brochure entitled "Contemporary Arab Studies Program at the Center for Middle Eastern Studies, Harvard University," p. 1. The newsletter announcement of the new program reported nothing whatsoever about the source of funding. "Contemporary Arab Studies Program Established at Harvard," *The Middle East at Harvard: The Newsletter of the Center for Middle Eastern Studies* 8 (Summer 1995), pp. 1–4.

34. Norvell B. DeAtkine, "The Middle East Scholars and the Gulf War," *Parameters* 23, no. 2 (Summer 1993), pp. 60–61.

35. Typical examples: a series of three workshops on "Defining the State in the Middle East," organized by Timothy Mitchell and Roger Owen, which met in Aix-en-Provence, Istanbul, and Oxford from 1988 through 1990; and a 1993 conference in Cairo, organized by Timothy Mitchell and Lila Abu-Lughod, on "Strategies for Post-Orientalist Scholarship on South Asia and the Middle East." The deliberations of these meetings, reported in thick jargon in the SSRC's newsletter *Items*, bordered on the unintelligible. Promised collected volumes never materialized.

36. Judith E. Tucker, "Middle East Studies in the United States," in *The Next Arab Decade: Alternative Futures*, ed. Hisham Sharabi (Boulder: Westview Press, 1988), pp. 315–16.

37. Steven Heydemann, "The Near and Middle East Research and Training Act: Background and Current Status," *MESA Newsletter* 13, no. 4 (November 1991), pp. 1, 4, 7; and in slightly modified form in *Items* 46, no. 1 (March 1992), pp. 6–8.

38. Steven Heydemann, "Update on the Near and Middle East Research and Training Program of 1992 (NMERTP)," *MESA Newsletter* 14, no. 4 (November 1992), p. 6.

39. "Near and Middle East 1998 Awards" (URL no longer available; information on file).

40. *Catalog of Federal Domestic Assistance*, "82.005: Foreign Language and Area Studies: U.S. Students and Scholars" (URL no longer available; information on file).

41. These figured in the titles of grants awarded between 1998 and 2000.

42. Heydemann, "The Near and Middle East Research and Training Act" (*Items* version), p. 6.

43. Stanley J. Heginbotham, "The National Security Education Program: A Review and Analysis," *Items* 46, nos. 2–3 (June–September 1992), pp. 17–23.

44. "Resolution passed by the MESA Board of Directors and presented to the MESA Membership for a Referendum Vote," *MESA Newsletter* 15, no. 1 (January 1993), p. 12.

45. Senator David Boren, speech to the Senate, October 16, 1991, *Congressional Record*, S14781.

46. "Update on the National Security Education Program," *MESA Newsletter* 16, no. 2 (May 1994), p. 8.

47. See the proposal by the National Partnership for Reinventing Government, Department of Education Recommendations and Actions, ED04: Consolidate National Security Education Act Programs, http://govinfo.library.unt.edu/npr/library/reports/ED4.html

48. Ann Mosley Lesch, "Promoting Academic Freedom: Risks and Responsibilities" (1995 Presidential Address), *MESA Bulletin* 30, no. 1 (July 1996), p. 6.

49. Stanley J. Heginbotham, "Round Up the Usual Suspects," *Bulletin of Concerned Asian Scholars* 29, no. 1 (January–March 1997), http://csf.colorado.edu/bcas/sympos/syheginb.htm (The author was vice president of the SSRC at the time the program emerged.)

50. "Sheep in Wolf's Clothing," *Chronicle of Higher Education*, April 7, 2000, p. A59.

51. Philip S. Khoury, "Current Developments and Future Directions in Middle Eastern Studies," *Frontiers* 6 (Fall 2000), www.frontiersjournal.com/back/six/khoury.htm

52. Rashid I. Khalidi, "Letter from the President," *MESA Newsletter* 16, no. 1 (February 1994), p. 2.

53. Jerrold D. Green, "Where are the Arabs?" *Survival* 40, no. 2 (Summer 1998), p. 177.

54. Anthony H. Cordesman, "Living with Saddam: Reshaping U.S. Strategy in the Middle East," Testimony to the United States Committee on Armed Services, March 25, 1998, www.csis.org/hill/ts032598.html

55. Prepared statement of John L. Esposito, June 24, 1985, Subcommittee on Europe and the Middle East of the Committee on Foreign Affairs, House of Representatives, *Islamic Fundamentalism and Islamic Radicalism* (Washington, D.C.: Government Printing Office, 1985), p. 19.

56. See Esposito's bio in Timothy D. Sisk, *Islam and Democracy: Religion, Politics, and Power in the Middle East* (Washington, D.C.: United States Institute of Peace, 1992), p. 80. The jacket of the first hardcover edition of *The Islamic Threat* also emphasized his role as a "consultant to the State Department."

57. Dr. John L. Esposito curriculum vitae, www.cmcu.net/JLE_CV.htm

58. Address by Robert H. Pelletreau to the Council on Foreign Relations, May 8, 1996, www.state.gov./www/current/middle_east/960508.html

59. United States Institute of Peace Grant SG-158-92, entitled "Democracy, Identity, and Conflict Resolution in the Islamic World."

60. This was the conference entitled "Political Islam in the Middle East: Its Regional and International Implications," March 2–3, 1994, the proceedings of which were published as John L. Esposito, ed., *Political Islam: Revolution, Radicalism, or Reform?* (Boulder: Lynne Rienner: 1997).

61. Edward W. Said, *Covering Islam*, rev. ed. (New York: Vintage Books, 1997), p. xx.

62. John L. Esposito, *The Islamic Threat: Myth or Reality?* (New York: Oxford University Press, 1992), p. 202.

63. Edward W. Said, "The Phony Islamic Threat," *New York Times Magazine*, November 21, 1993.

64. Rashid Khalidi, "Letter from the President," p. 2.

65. Rashid Khalidi, "Is There a Future for Middle East Studies?" (1994 Presidential Address), *MESA Bulletin* 29, no. 1 (July 1995), p. 5.

66. Philip S. Khoury, "Letter from the President: Global and Local Perspectives," *MESA Newsletter* 20, no. 2 (May 1998), p. 3.

The Cultivation of Irrelevance

Exact scientific knowledge of the Near East will, of course, be all but useless
if it is confined within [academic] circles; it must be made effective in the
life of the community at large, through the newspapers, the radio, and
all the channels of communication and decision which ramify through
our society.

—Committee on Near Eastern Studies (1949)[1]

Middle Eastern studies might have been forgiven their alienation from
Washington, had they been "effective in the life of the community at
large." In no other country did academia and the media interact so freely
and intensely as in America. Nowhere else did university administrations
offer so many incentives and rewards for engaging the private sector. Middle
Eastern studies would find no difficulty winning a hearing, if only their champions were prepared to engage influential constituencies beyond the campus.

Yet the isolation of Middle Eastern studies from the American public
deepened in parallel with their alienation from government. In fact, the two
forms of withdrawal went hand in hand, complementing and reinforcing
one another. Alas, the leaders of Middle Eastern studies failed to understand a fundamental truth: if scholars cut themselves off from a government
conducted by and for the people, they were bound to cut themselves off
from the people.

Abhorring a Vacuum

Theoretically, Middle Eastern studies had a mechanism for reaching a wider
public. Since the 1970s, a portion of each Title VI center grant had been
earmarked for "outreach," a requirement imposed by the government on all
federally funded area studies centers. Middle East centers customarily allocated 10 to 15 percent of their Title VI grants to "outreach," sums spent
mostly on the salaries of "outreach coordinators."

But "outreach" did not reach very far, for a very simple reason: senior
faculty abhorred it. In 1979, MESA noted that "few faculty members have
shown a real commitment to the programs."[2] Since senior faculty were not

willing to put their shoulders to the wheel, the job of "outreach" generally devolved upon junior faculty and graduate students, who felt the most comfortable interacting with the least-informed publics. In the only systematic survey, the "outreach coordinators" of nine Middle East centers ranked their principal "outreach" audiences in this order: secondary school educators, the general public, community groups, elementary school educators, and university faculty. The coordinators did not list media or business, the two most sophisticated and demanding constituencies outside of government.[3]

Because senior faculty avoided "outreach" duties, the campus-based programs had little to offer these more discriminating audiences, and most "outreach" consisted of basic lectures to school principals and video loans to community and church groups. Rashid Khalidi once scolded his colleagues for "being holier-than-thou about outreach," and warned that the Department of Education was "perfectly capable of telling when we are faking it as far as outreach is concerned."[4] It was doubtful this admonition had any effect. A few centers, located in major cities, had something to show for their "outreach" efforts, but "faking it" became part of the standard operating procedure of most Middle East centers. In 1979, MESA had questioned "whether working through regional studies centers is a cost-effective way of accomplishing the goal of disseminating foreign-area expertise among the general public."[5] Given the insularity of the academics, it was a legitimate question, and the answer plainly was "no."

While the professors "faked it," the think tanks progressively colonized the public domain. When Said wrote *Orientalism*, think tanks played a negligible role in interpreting the Middle East. But over the next twenty years, a few dozen individuals working out of think tanks managed to establish more public credibility on Middle Eastern affairs than the entire membership of MESA.

The new reality only dawned on MESA's members during the Gulf War. The university centers were flooded by calls from the media; Georgetown's Center for Contemporary Arab Studies responded to more than 2,000 requests from the media and public.[6] But the academics were distressed to discover the emergence of another class of experts, who contested academe's exclusive claims. Yvonne Haddad pointed to the shift in her MESA presidential address, in the midst of the Gulf crisis:

> It is clear that the press has its list of accredited authorities from research institutions independent of the academic structure, not only to provide expertise on the area but also to contextualize and define reality, generating the "spin" as to what are the legitimate questions to ask when interpreting events in the Middle East. Researchers from within the Washington beltway think tanks and former security officers have acquired a certain legitimacy in the eyes of the media as the experts on the Middle East, and are in obvious demand to expound on the present situation despite the fact that a few

have readily admitted that they have never been to the area or studied in any of our academic centers.[7]

James Bill was even more pointed, regretting that "many of the leading scholars have found their perspectives ignored and devalued by the public and by policymakers who are inundated by the uninformed, slanted and repetitious opinions of the instant experts." These "intellectual counterfeiters" and "pseudo-authorities" had achieved "considerable success in penetrating the policy-making apparatus in Washington, where their superficial and twisted analyses" harmed American interests and "reinforced the long-standing gap between knowledgeable well-trained scholars and policymakers."[8]

Nowhere did the academics pause to reflect on how the think tanks had acquired their clout. Back on campus, the academics comforted themselves in the thought that the think tanks flourished only because of their big money and organizational technique. "The influence of the contemporary Middle East studies network," complained one of MERIP's editors in 1997, "is dwarfed by the financial resources and institutional muscle of right-wing organizations intent on advancing an ethos of pro-Americanism of the most retrograde variety in the nation's public fora."[9]

But the money advantage was a myth. In fact, only one or two Middle East–specific think tanks approximated the annual cost of one of the top dozen university-based Middle East centers and their salaried faculty. Even the biggest general think tanks spent less on their Middle East programs than middle-range universities spent on theirs. The budgets devoted by universities, foundations, and government to maintaining more than a dozen National Resource Centers, 125 programs, and more than 2,000 professors dwarfed the combined expenditures of the think tanks.

Was it any more true, as Haddad claimed, that the think tank denizens were but instant experts, who had not studied in "our academic centers"? Disparaging the credentials of the think tankers became a favorite academic pastime. In 1993, Stanford's Joel Beinin wrote that one particularly successful think tank, The Washington Institute for Near East Policy, had gained its influence despite the "minimal involvement of scholars with substantive knowledge of the region."[10] It was comforting for the new mandarins to think that no such "substantive knowledge" existed outside their carefully patrolled perimeters.

But these claims could not withstand closer scrutiny. True, in the think tanks—as in the universities—not everyone was the expert he or she pretended to be. But in the 1980s and 1990s, the intolerant climate in academe had driven many talented people with "substantive knowledge" into the more diverse and open world of the think tanks. There they dramatically raised the level of Middle East–related research, which often surpassed university-based research in clarity, style, thoroughness, and cogency. Nor was there anything "instant" about their academic credentials. For example, in 1993, the very institute derided by Beinin named as director an academic (Robert Satloff) who had completed his doctorate at Oxford (under Roger Owen). Its senior fellow in military affairs (Michael Eisenstadt) had his master's degree in Arab studies from Georgetown.

The success of the think tanks ultimately depended on neither money nor "muscle." It sprang from an ability to formulate and present ideas in the accepted public discourse of the national interest. Only a handful of people in academe, such as John Esposito and, to a lesser extent, Augustus Richard Norton, knew how to do this, and their paradigms had turned out to be substantively wrong. The growing reputation of the think tanks rested on their delivery of timely, reliable, and persuasive analyses of developments and trends that bore on the interests and policies of the United States.

There was an almost schizophrenic contradiction between the academics' refusal to do such work themselves, and their jealous resentment of those outside academe who did it. "Should we learn to operate within their circles," asked Haddad, "to hone our skills, to make pithy soundbites in order to have more input into America's understanding of the Middle East? Or should we devote ourselves to serious research and leave the task of popular interpretation to others?"[11] The answer, for the vast majority of academics, was to leave it to others—and then complain about them in their faculty lounges.

Even more humiliating to the guild was the growing prominence of independent journalists and writers. Said had derided the journalists in *Covering Islam*, and a general contempt for them pervaded the academy. Rashid Khalidi, while president of MESA, vented a widespread resentment against the influence of journalists and writers. "[On the] level of policy and public discourse," he wrote to MESA members, "we who actually know something about the Middle East, and have been there, and know the languages, are largely ignored, while ill-informed sensationalists like Steven Emerson and Robert D. Kaplan hog the headlines and grace the podiums of think-tanks and lecture halls."[12] In fact, many journalists were extremely well informed (and well travelled), and even controversial ones often unearthed important information. But whatever one thought of the journalists on Middle Eastern beats, their rise had been made easier by the deliberate refusal of academics to engage the press.

Roger Owen personified this retreat. In the midst of another Middle East crisis, Owen found time to write a short piece—for an Egyptian weekly. There he rationalized his disengagement from the American debate. "Given the very narrow political parameters which govern any policy towards the Middle East," he wrote, there was "little mileage to be gained by running campaigns to convince those in Washington." As for the media, "journalists who try to find out my opinions are so ignorant themselves that I cannot reasonably trust any of them to report what I try to say correctly." Owen's conclusion? "It is better, for the moment, to spend my time with those of my students who are troubled and upset by both the crisis itself and by having to experience it here in these unfriendly surroundings. University teach-ins and workshops will follow."[13] (For the A. J. Meyer Professor of Middle Eastern History at Harvard, those "unfriendly surroundings" were these United States.) Countless academics made the same choice Owen did. It was much easier to huddle with student disciples, who constituted a subordinate class, indebted to and dependent on their professors in every conceivable way. Unlike journalists, they would hang on every word uttered by their mentors. After all, their careers might depend on it.

The crisis in Middle Eastern studies arose partly from this self-imposed isolation, and the loss of an ability to communicate beyond the field—something at which the pioneers of the field had excelled. The new guard, dancing to every new academic tune, found it ever more difficult to communicate with other Americans who had an interest in the region. Perhaps this was inevitable: the academics were intent upon winning legitimacy within the disciplines, even if this dictated obeisance to the gods of theory and shunning the vulgar media. But the disciplines, it turned out, were not so easily appeased.

Erosion of the Base

From their inception in the 1950s, area studies had academic critics within the disciplinary departments of the universities. These critics argued that the work done in area studies remained isolated from the main currents of the disciplines. In 1963, the imported knight of Middle Eastern studies, Sir Hamilton Gibb, warned that area studies could "never establish a claim to academic representation in the fields of the social sciences until its representatives give proof of matching academic quality within those fields. Nothing will more effectively discredit it than to become a haven for second- or third-class historians or sociologists."[14] In the case of Middle Eastern studies, Gibb's words proved prescient.

The leaders of Middle Eastern studies admitted as much, decade after decade. "The standing of most specialists in the eyes of their disciplinary colleagues is not very high," acknowledged Leonard Binder in 1976.[15] Social science research devoted to the Middle East had "failed to produce innovative or pathbreaking results," admitted political scientist (and later AUB president) John Waterbury in 1985; it "has tended to be imitative, occasionally deficient, and all too frequently uninteresting."[16] In 1994, Rashid Khalidi pointed to "the increasing tendency of the Middle East field to be out of touch with important current trends in some disciplines. . . . [S]ome sectors of the Middle East field are retrograde either in contrast to the study of other regions or in terms of the advances in certain disciplines."[17]

This last admission was perhaps the weightiest: Middle Eastern studies were "retrograde" even in comparison with other area studies. Sometimes the testimony came from outside the field, as it did from Lucien Pye, a critic of all area studies, in 1975: "Of all the regions of the world, historically scholarship on the Middle East has been possibly the most remote from the mainstream of political science."[18] At other times, the admission came from inside the field: "Area studies focusing on Latin America, Sub-Saharan Africa, and South Asia," wrote Waterbury in 1985, "have been far more productive in generating findings and paradigms of relevance to their disciplines as a whole."[19]

Despite this record, major universities continued to host Middle Eastern studies, for three reasons. First, they enjoyed external financial support. It was difficult to spurn an enterprise that opened the purses of foundations and the government. Second, courses in Middle Eastern studies drew undergraduate enrollments, especially when the Middle East figured in the news as a trouble spot. Third, Middle Eastern studies, like all area studies, gave host universities an internationalist reputation. Area studies appealed to the institutional vanity of higher administrators, who thought that a university of top rank should cover the globe. And so for decades, Middle Eastern studies flourished through the good times and survived through the bad, despite the ambivalence of disciplinary departments.

But area studies remained potentially vulnerable, and the marginality of Middle Eastern studies made them potentially the most vulnerable of all area studies—were area studies ever to lose any of their supporting rationales. In the mid-1990s, this is exactly what happened.

Globalization Blues

As the century rushed to a close, dramatic events called into question the old rationales for area studies. The Soviet Union vanished, and with it disappeared the strategic partition that had defined world areas. The rending of the Iron Curtain suggested that no border could resist penetration by the forces of globalization. Goods, money, information, people—no checkpoint could block their flow, no national government could stem their tide. Global knowledge trumped culture-based knowledge in the marketplace; digital language became the global *lingua franca*. The world had changed, and these changes were grouped under the vast rubric of globalization. What was the point, then, of organizing American knowledge of the world around the unstable, indefinable, porous, and perhaps archaic entities known as "areas"?

In 1996, Kenneth Prewitt, president of the New York–based Social Science Research Council, issued an *ex cathedra* statement on area studies. For fifty years, the SSRC had been the conceptual godfather of all area studies, Middle Eastern studies included. The council set research agendas, mediated between academics and foundations, made appointments to its prestigious area committees (including one devoted to the "Near and Middle East"), and awarded much-coveted fellowships. The SSRC's commitment to area studies had survived many ups and downs of foundation and government support.

But the SSRC could not resist the globalization bandwagon. Prewitt paid his respects to the past achievements of area studies; they were "the most successful, large-scale interdisciplinary project ever in the humanities and the social sciences." But the world had "been shaken loose from its familiar moorings" by globalization. Area studies—and, more to the point, the SSRC's area committees—were "not the optimum structure for providing new insights and theories suitable for a world in which the geographic units of analysis are neither static nor straightforward."[20] Before the year was out, the SSRC had effectively disbanded the area committees, replacing them with various "networks," "committees," "panels," and "working groups," organized thematically or functionally.[21] The Ford Foundation gave its blessing and backing to the shift, and also created its own program to assist in the retooling of area studies.[22]

The SSRC's exit from area studies was very different from the Ford Foundation's retreat thirty years earlier. The Ford Foundation had withdrawn because area studies seemed successful. They had taken firm root in the universities, and they could survive without the prop of massive foundation support. When the SSRC withdrew, it did so because area studies looked exhausted. These studies, so the council concluded, did not begin to address the kinds of questions posed by a globalized world. Priorities could not turn on a dime, but the message from New York was clear: the great days (and dollars) of area studies were finished.

For the comfortably tenured, the decision of the SSRC had few implications. But for their graduate students, it threatened trouble. Not only did the grants disappear; as one critic of area studies put it, departmental chairs could "now apply disciplinary criteria, rather than area knowledge, in evaluating and rewarding professional contributions."[23] In Middle Eastern studies, a net loss of positions seemed a very likely outcome.

Had the new leaders of Middle Eastern studies been made of sterner stuff, they would have risen to the defense of their "area." After all, a strong case could be made that the Middle East still constituted an efficient, and even essential, framework of analysis. The region remained an anomaly that begged explanation. Authoritarianism, monarchy, and religion all continued to dominate the politics of the Middle East in ways that defied rational-choice analysis, econometric models, and game theory. Concepts manufactured in the theory mills of North America broke down in the rugged environment of Saddam's Iraq or the Taliban's Afghanistan. The region's conflicts also defied resolution, and lingered on as endemic feuds. Many parts of the Middle East remained bastions against globalization and fell back on culture as a strategy of resistance. Surely this anomaly was worth understanding in its own terms. And who could best interpret it, if not those scholars who drew upon specialized and localized knowledge?

But the new masters of the guild could not make this argument systematically, precisely because they had seized power by making the *opposite* argument. Twenty years earlier, they had argued *against* the erudite mastery of languages, histories, cultures, and societies. It was sufficient to come armed with the right theory, the most universally valid paradigm, and then apply it to the Middle East. The idea that there was anything exceptional about the Middle East was diagnosed as a symptom of "latent" orientalism, a career-threatening affliction.

But if the Middle East was no exception, then why should department chairs make an exception and hire specialists on the region? In university after university, department chairs were quite content to dispense with Middle Eastern expertise altogether. As the leaders of the field became eager to prove that the Middle East remained somehow relevant to the shifting tides of academic priorities, they proposed three broad strategies of "revitalization," each one answering one of the common criticisms of area studies.

The borders of the Middle East seemed arbitrary and narrow? Expand the definition of the Middle East. Middle East specialists studied the region in isolation? Compare the Middle East to other world areas. Other area studies had cooperative relationships with institutions in their area? Build up cooperative relations with institutions and individuals in the region. Here was the three-part prescription by the field's leaders for revitalizing Middle Eastern studies in an age of globalization. Unfortunately, implementing each part was well beyond the capabilities of Middle Eastern studies as they had evolved over the previous twenty years.

Redefining the "Middle East"

The simplest proposed adjustment involved expanding the definition of the Middle East. As it had been defined through the Cold War, the region included the Arab world, Israel, Turkey, Iran, and sometimes Afghanistan. From an American Cold War perspective, the importance of the Middle East resided in its strategic position on the flank of the Soviet Union. With the end of the Cold War, the Middle East lost much of its strategic significance, although oil, Israel, and the danger of proliferation guaranteed a continuing American interest.

But if the definition of the Middle East were expanded, might Middle Eastern studies grow in relevance and resources? The most obvious direction of expansion was northward. After the collapse of the Soviet Union, the former Soviet republics of the Caucasus and Central Asia became independent states. Some of these states were rich in oil and gas, and most them were populated by Muslim peoples speaking Turkic languages. The study of these new states was poised for dramatic expansion. If Middle Eastern studies could colonize this region academically—defining it as part of a "greater Middle East"—might this not provide a much-needed boost for the field? As Philip Khoury, a former MESA president, pointed out, "the hunt for oil in the Caspian Sea and elsewhere in Central Asia is reinvigorating the study of the political economy of oil, which has a long tradition in Middle Eastern studies."[24]

But by the end of the 1990s, the institutions of Middle Eastern studies had failed to bring Caucasian and Central Asian studies under their umbrella. In part, this reflected the much more significant failure of Middle Eastern states to bring the region into their orbit. Scholars who predicted the emergence of a "greater Middle East" upon the breakup of the Soviet Union were disappointed. But it also reflected an underlying weakness in American-style Middle Eastern studies. That weakness showed itself in the inability of Middle East programs to keep even the Middle East under one academic umbrella.

The founders had believed strongly in the interdependence of the Arab, Persian, and Turkish subcultures of Islam. None could be understood in isolation from the other two, and American programs worked toward the symbiotic integration of the three. But beginning in the 1970s, the governments of Arab states, Iran, and Turkey offered funds for the establishment of programs devoted to their own subregions. Programs for Iranian and Turkish studies, each devoted to only the one country, usually remained within the framework of existing Middle East programs and centers. But Arab governments often preferred completely separate frameworks, and some universities were eager to accommodate them.

The separatism of "Arab studies" rested on the notion that this area had been somehow neglected. The initiators of Georgetown's Center for Contemporary Arab Studies, established in 1975, declared themselves "astounded to discover" that other Middle East programs offered "not a single course dealing specifically with governments or political systems of the Arab world."[25] In other programs, "work on the modern and contemporary periods tended to neglect the Arab world."[26] In fact, such "discoveries" were completely imaginary: the study of Arabic and Arab peoples, past and present, was the pillar of Middle Eastern studies in America from the very outset. But large foreign gifts gave academic Arabists the opportunity to create separate empires where they could pursue their own agendas in splendid isolation. At Georgetown, they did just that, and by the 1990s, money from Arab sources persuaded other universities to follow suit. In 1995, Harvard established a "Contemporary Arab Studies Program," and in 1998, Berkeley created the "Sultan Program in Arab Studies," named after a Saudi prince. The Sultan Program was intended to promote something called "Arab area studies."[27]

No wonder Middle Eastern studies did not have the wherewithal to "colonize" Caucasian and Central Asian studies. Academic Balkanization was dividing the Middle East itself into ever smaller units of study. The claims made by Jewish studies programs on the study of Israel and modern Hebrew had already taken them out of the orbit of Middle East programs and centers.[28] But the emergence of "Arab studies" threatened the very core of Middle Eastern studies, which seemed headed toward breakdown into a cluster of ethnic studies—hardly the ideal response to globalization.

Comparisons and Cooperation

If salvation did not lie in expanding the definition of the Middle East, might it be found in comparing the Middle East to other world areas? There had always been a measure of implicit or explicit comparison in Middle Eastern studies: specifically, comparisons of the Middle East to the West. But the post-orientalists denounced this comparison as an orientalist ruse, since it so often pointed to what the Middle East lacked. It was deployed in order to depict the Middle East as one of the "'not yet' societies—not yet democratic, not yet industrial, not yet civil, and so on."[29] What sort of comparison could avoid measuring the Middle East by a Eurocentric yardstick? The answer: comparison with South Asia.

South Asia was appealing because it shared with the Middle East a history of colonial rule and anticolonial resistance—and because postcolonial theory, inspired by Edward Said, had made the deepest inroads there. As Philip Khoury wrote, "Middle East specialists today are increasingly interested in testing postcolonial theory in their region and are looking for useful comparisons with South Asia."[30] In the 1990s, conferences comparing the Middle East with South Asia proliferated—all, of course, surrounded by the impenetrable fog of postcolonial theory. In 1993, the SSRC sponsored a meeting on "Strategies for Post-Orientalist Scholarship on South Asia and the Middle East." ("Modernity is a discourse in drag," declaimed one participant. "It is always cross-dressed.")[31] The trendsetters at New York University, a post-orientalist bastion, turned this meeting into a permanent working group, which in 1999 organized a conference on "comparative theoretical questions concerning the problem of modernity in South Asia and the Middle East."[32] In 2001, the University of California at Santa Barbara (host to a newly baptized Title VI center for the Middle East) launched a three-year project on "The Middle East and South Asia: Comparative Perspectives." The organizers promised to "rectify the drawbacks of traditional area studies by examining these two regions through comparative study."[33]

But did linkage to the supposedly theory-rich field of South Asian studies really constitute an option for most Middle East experts? Few were even familiar with the entire Middle East, let alone the complexities of South Asia. And did the Middle East and South Asia really share that much? The differences were just as striking as the supposed similarities—once one moved from postcolonial theory to postcolonial reality. One Arab intellectual came away from a visit to India absolutely stunned by the differences. "Why is it that the Arab world lags behind India?" he asked. "It does. Intellectually, we are not in the same world. There is a democracy in India. You can speak freely. People are not put in jail. The army has never been an important instrument of policy as it has been in, say, Pakistan, or virtually every single Arab country." It seemed unlikely that Middle East experts would want to pursue this unflattering line of comparison—even though it was drawn by none other than Edward Said himself.[34] An honest comparison with South Asia could only underline how much the Middle East *did* remain an exception. The comparison fad was unlikely to last very long.

The Myth of Indigenization

Or perhaps Middle Eastern studies could be revitalized through linkages to indigenous scholarship? After all, such cooperation had transformed other branches of area studies. Post-Soviet studies provided a striking example: "Kremlinology," resting on Cold War dichotomies, had been superseded by cooperative partnerships with institutions and individuals in the former Soviet Union. America's champions of Middle Eastern studies now called for such partnerships with their "colleagues" in Middle Eastern countries. Rashid Khalidi bravely looked to the East for agents of revitalization:

> Perhaps it is here, outside America and Europe, with their heavy institutional investments in both conservative Oriental studies and region-bound area studies, that an open-minded attitude to these processes that transcend specific areas of the world might be most easily found.

Khalidi averred that "scholars from the non-Western world have certain advantages with these new approaches and new fields which Western scholars do not have." They were "freer of some of the heavy intellectual and institutional baggage of rigid disciplines, inflexibly defined areas, and conservative departments." And they were "in immediate touch with many of the phenomena which we study from afar, and benefit from involvement in the debates within their societies."[35] These advantages extended to institutions. Roger Owen pledged to seek ways "of keeping in regular contact with Middle Eastern universities and research institutes as a way of identifying the key issues which will face the Arab world in the century to come."[36]

But did Middle Eastern scholars really enjoy "advantages" in "new approaches"? Were Arab scholars really "freer" than their Western colleagues? Were Arab institutions really more in touch with the "key issues" of the future? There was ample evidence that scholars in the Middle East labored under massive *dis*advantages, which ruined the prospect of any cooperation.

Manfred Halpern formulated the basic problem back in 1962: "The likely persistence in most of the Middle East of authoritarian regimes and of underpaid teachers and overcrowded universities without adequate freedom or resources will continue to inhibit important contributions from the area itself."[37] Some twenty years later, John Waterbury detected no improvement in the situation: "While the numbers may lie in the Arab world, it is not at all certain that the best research will be undertaken there. My own impression is that in general the political constraints on social science research have never been stronger."[38]

And in 1998, Rashid Khalidi completely contradicted himself, describing the state of scholarship in the Middle East in terms replicating Halpern's almost to the word: "The general picture is a grim one of grossly underpaid and overworked scholars, teaching huge numbers of students in overcrowded facilities, with poor research support and little access to international scholarship, operating under a variety of political and social pressures." Middle Easterners were eager to collaborate with Western scholars, noted Khalidi. But this collaboration, far from enriching Western scholarship with new insights, gravitated toward "flavor-of-the-month approaches imported from the West. What results is therefore often less collaboration than co-optation of regional social scientists."[39]

In short, salvation from the East was a pipe dream. Individuals and institutions in the region suffered from crippling disadvantages that ruled out meaningful cooperation. Indeed, it was all America's scholars could do to keep their foreign "colleagues" out of prison. In 1990, MESA established a Committee on Academic Freedom to protest infringements upon academic freedom in the Middle East. For the rest of the decade, MESA's *Newsletter* brimmed with letters to Middle Eastern governments, protesting the arrest or disappearance of academics and closures of universities and research institutions. The vulnerability of Arab social scientists came into sharp relief in 2000 in the case of the Egyptian sociologist Saad Eddin Ibrahim. The Arab world's most internationally prominent social scientist and a pioneer of cooperation with American scholars, was arrested, tried, and convicted by a government that received billions of dollars annually in U.S. aid. A decade after MESA took up the cause of such "colleagues," the prospect that cooperation with them might rescue Middle Eastern studies in America seemed more remote than ever.

Saved Once More

The field of Middle Eastern studies had "begun to rethink and even reinvent itself in the wake of the end of the Cold War and the spread of globalization"—so promised Philip Khoury.[40] But reinvention was much too strong a word to describe the modest strategies of Middle Eastern studies, and even these half-measures stood no chance of succeeding. They were devotional offerings meant to placate foundations and deans rather than genuine efforts to reinvent the field. Reinvention is a painful process, prompted by crisis; it is only undertaken when all measures of avoidance have been exhausted. And in Middle Eastern studies, there was neither pain nor crisis.

Why? Intellectual criticisms of area studies had no follow-up. Some of the reasons were bureaucratic: the institutions of area studies were too entrenched for their critics to effect any fundamental change. One historian of the Middle East attributed the resilience of area studies to "bureaucratic inertia," comparable to "what motivates NATO to carry on without a clear mission or a reason for existence, except, of course, for the mission of staying put or making itself bigger."[41] Perhaps the more important causes for this inertia were economic and demographic. Universities in the 1990s waxed rich as their endowment portfolios doubled, tripled, and quadrupled. They could also look forward to an enrollment boom, which stabilized faculty hiring. In this climate, it was easier to tolerate excess than to trim it.

No less important, government stood by area studies. From a practical point of view, the world had to be divided somehow, and the established divisions of area studies seemed as good as any. Nor was there any great pressure to trim government support: by the late 1990s, Washington debated not how to cut budgets, but how to spend surpluses. The Title VI entitlement, which had been a line item for forty years, survived the end of the Cold War without even a reassessment.

And so predictions of the death of area studies proved to be premature. "One would expect area studies to have become marginalized, if not practically extinct by now," concluded an observer in 1998. "Yet despite the initial panic over the SSRC's reorganization and the promises of massive cuts in the federal budget, there is little sign that we are actually moving towards such a point."[42] For Middle Eastern studies, this meant a new lease on the manor. As Khoury noted (with relief), the "post–Cold War budget cuts and the attack waged by the social science disciplines on area studies in the 1990s have not been as damaging to Middle Eastern studies as they were predicted to be."[43]

Relieved of any pressure, the mandarins took no initiative to debate future directions. When the founders faced an epistemological crisis in the mid-1970s, they had put MESA's shoulder to the wheel. The result was a series of meetings and papers that summarized the state of the field and considered future options. In the mid-1990s, the new leaders studiously avoided a comparable initiative. Such an exercise might have exposed the failings of the previous two decades and demonstrated how the new leaders had led Middle Eastern studies into a *cul-de-sac.* Such self-scrutiny was no longer the purpose of MESA; it had become a front organization, devoted to self-congratulation.

But the boosterism of MESA could not conceal the failure of the men and women who had led Middle Eastern studies for more than twenty years. They had erred in assessing the politics and societies of the Middle East.

They had fenced themselves off from effective interaction with government. They had cut themselves off from the general public. They had even lost the confidence of their colleagues in the disciplinary departments and their old friends in the foundations. Academic Middle Eastern studies had become irrelevant to everyone beyond them.

In the manner made popular by Edward Said, the academics blamed everyone but themselves. "The West feels that its stereotypes constitute 'knowledge' of the Middle East," complained one American political scientist on the pages of a leading journal. "Consequently there is an unwillingness to pay attention to scholarly analysis or even significantly support Middle East political teaching and research at the university level."[44] But the academics themselves, by perpetuating their own stereotypes of government, the media, and the public, had deliberately alienated themselves from every possible constituency but their peers. Middle Eastern studies under the post-orientalists had become a remote enclave of esoteric and irrelevant endeavor, resting on an ever-narrowing base of moral support.

Notes

1. Committee on Near Eastern Studies, *A Program for Near Eastern Studies in the United States* (Washington, D.C.: American Council of Learned Societies, 1949), p. 37.

2. "Statement of MESA on the Future of Federal Support for Foreign Area Studies," April 9, 1979, *MESA Bulletin* 13, no. 2 (December 1979), p. 111.

3. Kathleen Manning, *Outreach Educational Activities of Title VI National Resource Centers in International Studies: A Study Report with Recommendations* (Albany: Center for International Programs and Comparative Studies, State University of New York, 1983).

4. Rashid Khalidi, "Is There a Future for Middle East Studies?" (1994 Presidential Address), *MESA Bulletin* 29, no. 1 (July 1995), p. 3.

5. "Statement of MESA on the Future of Federal Support," p. 111.

6. 25th anniversary brochure of the Center for Contemporary Arab Studies, Georgetown University.

7. Yvonne Haddad, "Middle East Area Studies: Current Concerns and Future Directions" (1990 Presidential Address), *MESA Bulletin* 25, no. 1 (July 1991), p. 4.

8. James A. Bill, "The Study of Middle East Politics, 1946–1996: A Stocktaking," *Middle East Journal* 50, no. 4 (Autumn 1996), pp. 508–9.

9. Lisa Hajjar and Steve Niva, "(Re)Made in the USA: Middle East Studies in the Global Era," *Middle East Report* 7, no. 4 (October–December 1997), p. 6.

10. Joel Beinin, "Money, Media and Policy Consensus: The Washington Institute for Near East Policy," *Middle East Report* 23, no. 1 (January–February 1993), p. 12.

11. Haddad, "Middle East Area Studies," p. 4.

12. Khalidi, "Is There a Future for Middle East Studies?," p. 5.

13. *Al-Ahram Weekly*, November 16–22, 2000.

14. Sir Hamilton Gibb, *Area Studies Reconsidered* (London: School of Oriental and African Studies, University of London, 1963), p. 14.

15. Leonard Binder, "Area Studies: A Critical Reassessment," in *The Study of the Middle East: Research and Scholarship in the Humanities and Social Sciences*, ed. Leonard Binder (New York: Wiley, 1976), pp. 6–7.

16. John Waterbury, "Social Science Research and Arab Studies in the Coming Decade," in *The Next Arab Decade: Alternative Futures*, ed. Hisham Sharabi (Boulder: Westview, 1988), pp. 293–94.

17. Rashid I. Khalidi, "Letter from the President," *MESA Newsletter* 16, no. 1 (February 1994), p. 20. Khalidi once illustrated the deficit with an anecdote: "Recently, when reading applications for a major fellowship competition, I was struck by how much narrower the submissions by applicants in the Middle East field were by comparison with those by applicants from other fields. Indeed, to someone who was not a Middle East expert, much in these proposals was unintelligible, and as a result utterly uninteresting: it spoke to no universal concern, and shared no common language with the non-specialist reader." Khalidi, "Is There a Future for Middle East Studies?" p. 2.

18. Lucien W. Pye, ed., *Political Science and Area Studies: Rivals or Partners?* (Bloomington: Indiana University Press, 1975), p. 170.

19. Waterbury, "Social Science Research," pp. 293–94.

20. Kenneth Prewitt, "Presidential Items," *Items* 50, no. 1 (March 1996), pp. 15–18.

21. Kenneth Prewitt, "Presidential Items," *Items* 50 nos. 2–3 (June–September 1996), pp. 31–40.

22. Joyce Mercer, "The Ford Foundation Shifts Its Focus and Structure," *Chronicle of Higher Education*, August 15, 1997; Ford Foundation, *Crossing Borders: Revitalizing Area Studies* (New York: Ford Foundation, 1999).

23. Robert H. Bates, "Area Studies and the Discipline: A Useful Controversy?" *PS: Political Science and Politics* 30, no. 2 (June 1997), p. 167.

24. Philip S. Khoury, "Current Developments and Future Directions in Middle Eastern Studies," *Frontiers* 6 (Fall 2000), www.frontiersjournal.com/back/six/khoury.htm

25. John Ruedy, "Center Finds Its Academic Niche in Focus on Politics, History, and International Relations," *CCAS News* (September 1995), p. 1.

26. Michael C. Hudson, "CCAS Celebrates 20 Years of Quality Education on the Modern Arab World," *CCAS News* (September 1995), p. 7.

27. "The Sultan Endowment for Arab Studies," *Center for Middle Eastern Studies Newsletter, University of California at Berkeley* 20, no. 2 (Spring 1999), p. 1.

28. For the separate history of this field, see Paul Ritterband and Harold S. Wechsler, *Jewish Learning in American Universities: The First Century* (Bloomington: Indiana University Press, 1994).

29. Joel S. Migdal and John T. S. Keeler, "Bridging the Divide," *Items* 47, no. 4 (December 1993), p. 88.

30. Khoury, "Current Developments."

31. Timothy Mitchell and Lila Abu-Lughod, "Questions of Modernity," *Items* 47, no. 4 (December 1993), p. 83. The author of this particular insight is not named.

32. www.nyu.edu/gsas/program/neareast/6_working_groups.html

33. E-mail conference announcement by Dwight Reynolds, February 19, 2001.

34. Interview with Edward Said, *al-Jadid* 22 (Winter 1998), p. 29.

35. Rashid Khalidi, "The 'Middle East' as a Framework of Analysis: Re-Mapping a Region in the Era of Globalization," *Comparative Studies of South Asia, Africa and the Middle East* 18, no. 1 (1998), pp. 79–80.

36. "Contemporary Arab Studies Program Established at Harvard," *The Middle East at Harvard: The Newsletter of the Center for Middle Eastern Studies* 8 (Summer 1995), p. 3.

37. Manfred Halpern, "Middle Eastern Studies: A Review of the State of the Field with a Few Examples," *World Politics* 15, no. 1 (October 1962), p. 119.

38. Waterbury, "Social Science Research," p. 298.

39. Rashid Khalidi, "The Social Sciences in the Middle East," *Items* 52, nos. 2–3 (June–September 1998), p. 47.

40. Khoury, "Current Developments."

41. Reşat Kasaba, "Towards a New International Studies," last updated September 25, 1998, http://jsis.artsci.washington.edu/programs/is/toanewis.html

42. Ibid.

43. Khoury, "Current Developments."

44. Louis J. Cantori, "Democracy, Islam, and the Study of Middle Eastern Politics: Introduction," *PS: Political Science* 27, no. 3 (September 1994), p. 507.

Conclusion: When Gods Fail

Middle Eastern studies in America over the last quarter of a century did not so much focus on a particular subject of study or inquiry as they sought ways of testing certain methodological schemes and theoretical hypotheses. In the process, the theories somehow acquired divine attributes and status, and young practitioners came to worship at their various altars at different stages or periods. Since then there have been several gods of Middle Eastern studies in America that failed.

—*P. J. Vatikiotis (1978)*[1]

Little could the author of these words have imagined how many more gods of Middle Eastern studies would fail over the next quarter of a century. Confident theories about political Islam and "civil society"—the great orthodoxies of Middle Eastern studies in the 1980s and 1990s—stood in ruins by the year 2000. The work of a generation had come to naught.

The failed generation was formed by three moments of enthusiasm: 1958, 1968, and 1978. At each moment, eager graduate students and newly minted professors thought they felt the beating wings of history, the beginning of some new and liberating epoch in the long saga of the Middle East. Henceforth, things would be different and better: this was the lesson the young idealists drew from each moment. But it was the wrong lesson, each and every time.

The oldest of the mandarins experienced the exhilarating apogee of Arab nationalism in 1958. Surely, they concluded, nothing could resist the power of the surging masses in their demand for unity and revolution. The foreign enthusiasts of Arab nationalism were soon disappointed, but they would be marked thereafter by a chronic weakness for the "Arab street," which trumped all other factors in their analyses.

In 1968, another surging mass, this time Palestinian, captured the imagination of young academics, many of them Arab-Americans. The Palestinians would make the revolution that Nasser had failed to make, and they would break the old order in the Middle East, just as the 1968 generation in the United States broke the old order of the American campus. The moment came—and went. Yet even as the Palestinian revolution ground to a halt, its academic enthusiasts continued to anticipate its resurgence at any moment. Nothing caused greater fury than its repeated frustration.

In 1978, the Iranian revolution combined with publication of Edward Said's *Orientalism* to put the finishing touches on the new orthodoxy. Iran's revolution finally proved that the masses could topple a powerful regime—although they did it in the name of the wrong cause, a retrograde reading of Islam. Never mind: all the enthusiasm once invested in Arabism was now shifted to Islamism, which took its place as the irresistible force for liberation, the motor of reform, the fulcrum of "civil society." In time, Islamism would reveal itself to be none of these things. But in the two decades that followed Iran's revolution, susceptibility to the claims of Islamism became part of the standard gear of the American academic.

It was Said's *Orientalism* that gave ideological coherence to these expectations of liberation. Said fortified the new generation with the argument that an orientalist conspiracy had concealed the forces of change. Once orientalist cobwebs were swept away, the truth would become self-evident: the Muslims in general, and the Arabs in particular, were on an unstoppable victory march to revolution, liberation, and democracy. The post-orientalists, fired by their conviction and buoyed by the surge of the student left into the faculty ranks, took over the institutions of Middle Eastern studies. They controlled the Middle East centers, MESA, and the foundation panels. And there they waited for the Middle East to catch up to them.

It never did. For this generation, the balance of their century came as a crushing disappointment. Nothing unfolded according to expectation, nothing conformed to theory. Weaned on the certainty of change from below, the new generation had to interpret decade after decade of political immobility and economic stagnation, the empowerment of the state and the demobilization of society. History had dealt the academics a bad hand. Even worse, they tried to play their deuces as though they were aces, destroying their credibility in the process. Over time, they forfeited the trust of government, the public, the foundations, and even their own departments.

Reform from Within?

One could end a critique of Middle Eastern studies in America right here. The story would then have a beginning, middle, and end. An academic establishment tried to explain and predict change in a part of the world important to the United States. It failed to do so persuasively and accurately. Other institutions took up the slack, leaving the academics to debate one another in growing obscurity.

If the Middle East had lost its importance to the United States, one could leave it at that. But the Middle East continues to preoccupy Americans. Whether the subject is energy or human rights, missile defense or nuclear proliferation, Iran or Iraq, Islamism or Israel, terrorism or weapons of mass destruction, the Middle East engenders public debate and compels policymaking at the highest levels. Indeed, it is one of the few parts of the world where the United States could find itself even more deeply involved over the next two decades. American understanding of the Middle East—an understanding in perpetual need of improvement—could still be enhanced by an improvement in the performance of Middle Eastern studies.

What will it take to heal Middle Eastern studies, if they can be healed at all? The usual mantra among academics is that the field has to submit even more reverentially to the disciplines and their theories. The mandarins proclaim that "scholars of Middle East politics must prove their credentials by the demonstrable theoretical relevance of their work," in the first instance by "showing that generally available theoretical claims and categories are applicable in Middle Eastern settings."[2]

These theories are powerful totems—far more powerful than the realities of the Middle East, which are distant and remote from the American campus. In such a climate, there is a strong incentive to put theoretical commitments before empirical observation. Even though this has been the source of repeated error, breaking out of the circle involves professional risk of a high order. To put the Middle East before theorizing about the Middle East is to run the risk of being denounced as a disciplinary naïf or a "latent" orientalist. In striking contrast, there is no professional cost for substantive error in interpreting the actual Middle East. Indeed, leaders of the field do it all the time without any negative consequences.

Yet the salvation of Middle Eastern studies lies precisely in looking past the rapid turnover of theories in the social sciences to the Middle East itself in all its theory-defying complexity. Certainly this must be the lesson of the debacles of the last twenty years, all of which originated precisely in the effort to slavishly apply irrelevant or faulty paradigms to the region. The academics are naturally reluctant to cast Middle Eastern studies as a spoiler of the social sciences, and it is always safer to take a seat in the chorus. But reducing the Middle East to a set of proofs will not only perpetuate the marginality of Middle Eastern studies. It will rob the field of its potential for contributing to the great debates, present and future, over the place of the Middle East in a globalized world.

Nor will Middle Eastern studies in America pull out of the doldrums if their leaders persist in totally negating the very rich patrimony of scholarly orientalism. For all the limitations of this tradition, it inculcated high standards of cultural literacy and technical proficiency. It also cultivated an appreciation of the uniqueness of Islamic civilization in its Middle Eastern setting. As a result, the study of Islam in the orientalist tradition enjoyed cultural prestige. Its greatest practitioners commanded respect throughout their own societies and among learned Middle Easterners. In contrast, the post-orientalists have made Middle Eastern studies into a mere dependency of the social sciences and relegated themselves to the dubious duty of proving the universality of the latest theories propounded by the trendiest academic celebrities. Orientalism had heroes. Middle Eastern studies have none, and they never will, unless and until scholars of the Middle East restore some continuity with the great tradition.

The obstacles to this shift are formidable. The field of Middle Eastern studies is strewn with living monuments to recent excesses. Walk down the hall of any Middle East center, read the names on the doors, and recall the controversies and fads of America at end-of-century. Not everyone can be reinvented, not everyone can reinvent. But Americans reinvented Middle Eastern studies at least twice before, forty years ago in response to Title VI, and twenty years ago in response to the appearance of *Orientalism*. Middle Eastern studies are due for another reinvention.

As in the past, so this time, it is generational change that will renew and reinvigorate the field. The mission will probably be accomplished by people who are under forty, who are not implicated in the excesses of the recent past, and who understand how perilously close to the precipice they have been led. Their task will be a formidable one. The climate that now prevails in Middle Eastern studies is best described in these words:

> A young scholar depends on this network for his or her subventions, to say nothing of employment and the possibility of publication in the established journals. To venture unfriendly critiques of the recognized scholars or of their work, in this field more than in the fields of general history or literature, is to risk too much. . . . And the moment a voice is heard that challenges this conspiracy of silence, ideology and ethnic origins become the main topic.[3]

This was Edward Said, writing in 1981. Are these words any less true today, now that Said's disciples govern Middle Eastern studies? It might even be said that they are truer than ever.

The role of the secure, senior scholars is therefore crucial. They now have the obligation of going back to ask how and why they went wrong. Lisa Anderson and James Bill, political scientists, had the standing and the courage to admit that they and their colleagues persistently failed to explain the Middle East. The regeneration of Middle Eastern studies will proceed more rapidly if more senior scholars come forward from all of the disciplines, to debate and criticize the state of the field and reexamine the validity of their own theories, paradigms, and methodologies.

To the founders' credit, they did just that twenty-five years ago, when their own constructs began to fail. At that time, Leonard Binder, as MESA president, mobilized the now-defunct Research and Training Committee of MESA to analyze the state of the field. Even Said found merit in the resulting book, *The Study of the Middle East* (1976), precisely because it revealed Middle Eastern studies to be "an embattled field," surrounded by "a general air of crisis."[4]

Where is the air of crisis today? The leaders of Middle Eastern studies instead radiate smugness, shake their heads at the tumult in the public arena, and retreat ever more deeply into their own secluded world, with its rigid etiquette of theory and its peculiar mannerisms of political posturing. Complacency pervades the senior ranks. Today it is almost impossible to imagine MESA, under such leadership, initiating a collective soul searching. MESA now functions as a kind of union or lobby that boosts the image of Middle Eastern studies and circles the wagons against any criticism.

What about those supposed hothouses of innovation, the Social Science Research Council and the Ford Foundation? The SSRC, which marched Middle Eastern studies down every dead end in the 1980s and 1990s, has now convened a "Regional Advisory Panel" for the Middle East and North Africa, to survey the state of the field around the world and "set up new and different kinds of networks between scholars who work on the region."[5] Its opening gambit has been to ponder whether there even is a Middle East to study—yet another inauspicious beginning on Third Avenue. As for the Ford Foundation, it has become a virtual colony of the most radical post-orientalists. In 1997, the foundation entrusted the post-orientalist fashion designers at New York University with developing a "demonstration model for renewing the field of Middle Eastern studies."[6] Ford's most recent major contribution to the field, made in 1999, was a $300,000 grant to the "progressive" activists of MERIP, the "leftover left," to enable them "to reach a wider audience in the media, policy and education arenas."[7] In its dogged pursuit of the latest trend, Ford is often the first foundation to put its money down. And it is usually the last foundation to acknowledge its losses.

The next breakthroughs will not come from within these institutions. The professional associations and the big foundations, where rewards derive solely from adherence to consensus, are notoriously slow at responding to changing reality. The breakthroughs will come from individual scholars, often laboring on the margins. As the dominant paradigms grow ever more elaborate, inefficient, and insufficient, they will begin to shift. There will be more confessions by senior scholars, and more defections by their young protégés. The question is whether anything can or should be done from outside academe to accelerate the process.

The Title VI Conundrum

Were Middle Eastern studies strictly an academic hobby, it would be possible to sit back and watch their slow evolution with hope, trepidation, or bemusement. But Middle Eastern studies are not a hobby, nor do they rely solely on university budgets and foundation largesse. The U.S. government continues to subsidize Middle Eastern studies, most significantly through the Title VI program and its designation of National Resource Centers on the Middle East. Should that subsidy continue?

On the face of it, Title VI may not seem crucial to the operation of Middle Eastern studies. Most of the members of MESA do not practice in Title VI centers, and they do not depend on any federal subsidy. There are also programs and centers that have never been funded under Title VI and centers that have lost Title VI funding for one reason or another. Even at the National Resource Centers, Title VI grants cover less than 10 percent of the actual cost of Middle Eastern studies, since the cost of professors' salaries is borne by the universities themselves. In quantitative terms, Title VI grants are no more than the capstone to a very broad-based pyramid of university support.

Nevertheless, the fate of Middle Eastern studies as a collective endeavor does depend in important ways on government. In fiscal year 2002, the average National Resource Center for the Middle East will receive $300,000 in Title VI grants and fellowships. The grants make possible everything from enhanced language instruction to international conferences, and the fellowships are even more important. It has been estimated that 70 percent of the Ph.D.s in Middle Eastern studies come from the Title VI centers.[8] "Though U.S. government funding has waxed and waned over the last 25 years," a historian has noted, "it remains today a fundamental element in the training of graduate students in all fields of Middle Eastern Studies."[9] Any cut in these funds, warns a past president of MESA, would have "a drastic impact."[10] And since the Title VI competition is the only ostensibly objective measure of the relative strength of centers, Title VI status can be leveraged to extract additional funds from universities and foundations. "The federal contribution to the maintenance of these studies is crucial," admitted MESA in a 1979 statement, "since it is symbolic of national commitment" and "encourages universities and outside funding sources to continue their support."[11]

Over the years, Title VI has been the most consistent and predictable source of outside funding for Middle Eastern studies. The foundations have been erratic, moving in and out of area studies according to prevailing fad and fashion. Middle Eastern governments have been fickle, giving sporadically when it suits some policy or public relations purpose. Disciplinary departments have been unpredictable, making Middle Eastern appointments only after other needs have been met—if they make them at all. Only Title VI has been there, year in and year out, for Middle Eastern studies. Its loss would be much more than an indignity.

The old argument for federal support rested on the relevance of the enterprise to the national interest. In 1979, MESA announced that Middle East programs "not only warrant continued support by virtue of their proven worth, but absolutely require it by virtue of their direct relation to the national interest. Much of our foreign policy and private foreign involvement at the present day is based either directly or indirectly upon the work of the last two generations of scholarship."[12] This argument was dubious then; it would be regarded as absurd today. The last thing Middle Eastern studies have sought to do this last quarter-century has been to serve American foreign policy or private initiative.

There are three rather more plausible arguments for government support of Middle Eastern studies. One is that the centers, in an inadvertent way, do train numbers of people for public service and the private sector. Despite the best-laid plans of the professors, the centers occasionally produce graduates who are not copies of their teachers. These resourceful souls filter out the biases and take away fundamental knowledge of the Middle East and its languages that they employ elsewhere. One encounters these graduates here and there, and each of them is a testament to an independence of thought that cannot be suppressed by even the most rigid of academic regimes. Support for Middle Eastern studies might well be justified by such accidents.

A second plausible argument is that such centers represent precisely the kind of indulgence that a great power can and should afford itself. A diplomat once described the Arabists of the Foreign Service as "the Pekinese orchids begot by an American superpower."[13] The same could be said of the Middle East centers today. Their existence is itself a cause for wonderment, a mark of America's unrivalled ability to sustain excess. They contribute nothing to American power, but they amply express it. They meet no practical need, yet the intricate, ornate, and baroque flourishes of the ideas they shelter both stimulate and provoke, even as we know them to be absurd.

This is not an insubstantial justification. The failings of Middle Eastern studies are themselves an object lesson in the limits of expertise, and it behooves a great power to sustain (yet ignore) an entire branch of scholarship merely to analyze its failures. If the analysis is done, and its lessons are not lost, the Middle East centers of Title VI may well represent a justifiable expenditure of $4 million a year—the cost of about five Tomahawk cruise missiles.

And this leads to the most persuasive argument of all: the sums provided for Middle Eastern studies are a pittance by Washington standards, and are a small premium to pay to keep some channel open to academe in anticipation of better times. All of Title VI has been described as "an international pimple on the face of a domestic giant."[14] And only one-tenth of the money for area centers and fellowships under Title VI is allocated to the Middle East. It would be unreasonable to expect government to delve into the state of any particular branch of area studies, given the minuscule sums at stake. And who knows? Middle Eastern studies could turn around.

Still, even pimples are not exempt from scrutiny in an accountable government, and Title VI is again under review. The 1993 Government Performance and Results Act (GPRA) requires that every federal program have rigorous evaluation procedures, including goals-performance indicators and reporting instruments, in place by 2001. The National Foreign Language Center (NFLC) has been contracted to evaluate Title VI (and Fulbright-Hays) in the context of "national needs," and will complete its work in 2003.

Many of the measures will quantify the kinds of work Title VI centers have always done in Ph.D. production and language instruction. But the project will also seek to quantify measures of academic-societal interaction that have not been quantified before. "Much knowledge and information about the world have been generated by the Title VI academic community," notes the NFLC's statement of strategic goals, "but there is evidence that it has not always been effectively transmitted to decisionmakers in the public and business spheres." Among other measures, the evaluation will quantify the "number of testimonies to legislative bodies and consultancies to the government and private sector by National Resource Center–supported scholars in areas critical to the national interest." And the evaluation will also seek to quantify the "annual number of activities for business, media, government, and the general public provided by National Resource Centers."[15] Once benchmarks are set for performance, all area studies centers will face a continuous requirement for improvement—one that Middle East centers will be hard-pressed to meet.

Modest Reforms

When all the quantification is finished, the question will become one of policy. The future of Title VI will depend on countless factors that cannot be elucidated here. But now that the private foundations and the academic disciplines have called area studies into question, it seems probable that government will (belatedly) do the same. There will be proposals to abolish Title VI, and counterproposals to reform it. In the past, all such debates have ended in some measure of reform, and it is likely that the battle will be fought on precisely this ground. If Middle Eastern studies were to serve as a kind of prototype for reform of Title VI, which corrections would contribute to meeting the "national need" of reconnecting the field to its external constituencies?

One practical and easy adjustment would be to reallocate points in the competitive selection process of National Resource Centers. As it stands, centers are evaluated by a scoring system, in areas largely related to the quality of academic programs, curriculum, staff, and library. Of 165 possible points, only 5 are awarded for "outreach" to business, media, and the general public. Government is not even mentioned.[16] As one recent study of outreach points out, academics assume that the Department of Education "assigns low priority to outreach—both in terms of the competition point system and the manner in which outreach is assessed and monitored."[17] The present point allocation reflects a narrow view of what constitutes "excellence" in a Middle East center, and offers minimal incentive for center faculty to reach out to influential constituencies beyond the campus. A shift in point allocation would be felt throughout Middle Eastern studies and would send a clear signal that "excellence" is also the ability to communicate with the American people.

A second practical way to make the field more responsive to knowledgeable and interested constituencies would be to widen the Title VI review process to include more nonacademics. As it stands, the selection of National Resource Centers is determined by "a peer review process involving broadly representative professionals."[18] Peer review is a vital element of academic life, and it has no substitute in the myriad internal procedures of academic appointments and promotions. But the selection of National Resource Centers should not be treated as an internal academic procedure if its purpose is to select those centers best placed to impart their "excellence" also beyond academe.

On these grounds, there would seem to be every reason to involve at least some government officials and other interested and knowledgeable citizens in the selection process. More than twenty years ago, a RAND report suggested the establishment of "new panels, comprising both specialists in the field and interested users of its talents—notably, government agencies, which are not necessarily represented on the relevant panels."[19] The participation of nonacademics would compel center directors to build bridges to constituencies beyond their guild, to assure themselves an advantage in those instances where the competition is close, as it usually is.

These modest measures would begin to encourage change in Middle Eastern studies, but implementing them would be difficult. Area studies are effectively unionized, and even the smallest procedural changes in Title VI cannot be implemented without assessing their impact upon all of the many other "stakeholders." Indeed, the structure of area studies is far more resilient than its rationales. Proposals for the reform of Title VI are highly suspect in academic eyes, and are inevitably countered by the full force of the entire higher education lobby.

In this light, it is important for Congress to take a deeper interest in Title VI, and Middle Eastern studies are as good a place as any to begin asking questions. A relevant congressional subcommittee might hold a hearing on the contribution of Middle Eastern studies to American public policy. The most obvious address would be the House Labor, Health and Human Services, and Education Appropriations Subcommittee, which holds hearings early each spring on the budget request of the Department of Education. Testimony might be invited from the officers of MESA and the directors of Title VI centers, but also from representatives of government departments and agencies, directors of think tanks, and independent-minded scholars, whose perspective is external to the enterprise. The effect of such a hearing would be to sensitize the academic recipients of taxpayer dollars to the concerns of the American people, expressed through their elected representatives. It would also provide an opportunity for the academics to convey their own concerns to government.

Reopening a Field

Changes in Title VI can help erode the culture of irrelevance that has pervaded Middle Eastern studies. But no amount of tweaking this program can cure the more fundamental ailments that afflict the field. This healing can only be achieved by the guild: the physicians must heal themselves.

Over the next decade, a new generation, formed in a very different world than their predecessors, will begin to redraw the parameters of the field. If they are to save Middle Eastern studies, they will have to cast aside the monopolizing practices of their teachers and actively promote intellectual diversity. Middle Eastern studies are already diverse in superficial ways: they are spread geographically across the country, and they are home to people of many ethnic and religious backgrounds. But they lack a culture of tolerance for diversity in ideas and approaches. This problem is inevitable in small and insular fields; it can be solved only by a deliberate effort to open Middle Eastern studies to debate. If the academics do not do this themselves, deans and provosts are likely to intervene with ever-increasing frequency. If younger scholars want to preserve the long-standing autonomy of Middle Eastern studies, they will have to run the risk of reopening the field. The Middle Eastern studies *nomenklatura* may be impossible to abolish, but it must permit opposition.

The new generation must also forge a different kind of relationship with the world beyond the campus. Middle Eastern studies must regain their relevance, or risk becoming "Exhibit A" in any future case against public support for area studies. They can best achieve this by rediscovering and articulating that which is uniquely American in the American approach to the Middle East. The idea that the United States plays an essentially beneficent role in the world is at the very core of this approach. So is a willingness to constructively engage one's own government and fellow citizens. This willingness need not imply the neglect of pure scholarship, a narrow nationalism, or even a renunciation of all Middle Eastern preferences. But it does imply that the scholar has a constituency outside the campus gates that deserves to be addressed.

It will take years for Middle Eastern studies to restore its reputation for credibility and relevance. But for better or worse, the Middle East provides frequent opportunities for its interpreters to test and prove themselves. It is not too late to begin anew.

Notes

1. P. J. Vatikiotis, "Middle Eastern Studies in America: A Memorandum," *Washington Review* 1, no. 1 (January 1978), p. 95.

2. Ian S. Lustick, "The Quality of Theory and the Comparative Disadvantage of Area Studies," *MESA Bulletin* 34, no. 2 (Winter 2000), p. 192.

3. Edward W. Said, *Covering Islam* (New York: Pantheon Books, 1981), p. 143.

4. Ibid., p. 133.

5. www.ssrc.org/programs/fellowprogram.cgi?Middle+East+and+North+Africa

6. Ford Foundation, *Crossing Borders: Revitalizing Area Studies* (New York: Ford Foundation, 1999), p. 34.

7. www.fordfound.org/grants_db/view_grant_detail.cfm?grant_counter=1121

8. Jere L. Bacharach, "The State of Middle Eastern Studies in Institutions of Higher Education in the U.S.," *MELA Notes* 62 (Spring 1995), p. 2.

9. R. Stephen Humphreys, "Tradition and Innovation in the Study of Islamic History: The Evolution of North American Scholarship since 1960," lecture presented at the University of Tokyo, October 21, 1997, www.l.u-tokyo.ac.jp/IAS/HP-e2/eventreports/humphreys.html#Humphreys

10. Ann Mosely Lesch, "Area Studies in Universities: Organization and Funding," in *Japan-USA Area Studies Conference*, ed. Matsubara Masatake and John Campbell, JCAS Symposium Series 1 (Osaka: Japan Center for Area Studies, 1997), p. 71.

11. "Statement of MESA on the Future of Federal Support for Foreign Area Studies," *MESA Bulletin* 13, no. 2 (December 1979), p. 110.

12. Ibid.

13. Hume Horan, quoted in Robert Kaplan, *The Arabists: The Romance of an American Elite* (New York: Free Press, 1993), p. 234.

14. Unnamed official quoted in Deborah Shapley, "Middle East Studies: Funding Wilts as Arab-U.S. Friendship Flowers," *Science* 185 (July 5, 1974), p. 43.

15. National Foreign Language Center, "National Resource Centers: Overview of Issues Regarding Performance Measures," www.nflc.org/activities/projects/eelias_nrc.htm

16. Code of Federal Regulations, Title 34, Chapter 6, Sec. 656.20-22.

17. John M. Metzler, "Challenges for Title VI Programs of Outreach in Foreign Language and International Studies," in *International Education in the New Global Era: Proceedings of a National Policy Conference on the Higher Education Act, Title VI, and Fulbright-Hays Programs*, ed. John N. Hawkins et al. (Los Angeles: International Studies and Overseas Program, University of California, Los Angeles, 1998), p. 119.

18. P.L. 105-244, Title VI, Sec. 607(c), www.ed.gov/legislation/HEA/sec601.html

19. Sue E. Berryman, Paul F. Langer, John Pincus, and Richard H. Solomon, *Foreign Language and International Studies Specialists: The Marketplace and National Policy* (Santa Monica, Calif.: RAND, September 1979), pp. 73–74.

Appendix

FY 2000–2002 National Resource Centers and Foreign Language and Area Studies Fellowships (FLAS) Program for the Middle East

	Projected Annual Funding	
	Centers	**FLAS**
Emory University (undergrad.)	$185,000	
Georgetown University	$179,000	$54,000
Harvard University	$195,000	$183,000
Ohio State University (undergrad.)	$188,500	$75,000
Princeton University and New York University (consortium)	$199,000 (jt.)	$159,000 (ea.)
University of Arizona (undergrad.)	$197,000	$123,000
University of California, Berkeley	$191,000	$123,000
University of California, Los Angeles	$192,000	$129,000
University of California, Santa Barbara	$175,334	$54,000
University of Chicago	$190,000	$171,000
University of Michigan		$75,000
University of Pennsylvania	$185,000	$75,000
University of Texas, Austin	$190,000	$102,000
University of Utah	$170,011	
University of Washington	$170,011	
Total annual funding	**$2,606,856**	**$1,482,000**

Source: International Education and Graduate Service Program, U.S. Department of Education, CFDA 84.015A 84.015B

Index of Scholars and Institutions

This finder is intended as an aid in locating scholars, programs, universities, foundations, and government agencies. When a person is quoted but not explicitly named in the text, the page reference to the quote comes under the person's entry *in italics*. (All quotations are fully referenced in the endnotes.)

R

RAND, 1, 19, 63, 87, 96, 128
Research and Training Committee (of MESA), 19, 22, 123
Robinson, Glenn, 75–76, 82n53
Rockefeller Foundation, 11–12, 99n5
Rodinson, Maxime, 30–31, 35, 38
Roy, Olivier, 55
Ruedy, John, *112*
Rushdie, Salman, 45, 47, 58n14

S

Sadowski, Yahya, 61
Safran, Nadav, 89–90
Said, Edward, 2–3, 27–40, 40n3, 40n6, 41n13, 42n44, 44–52, 57n5, 58n10, 58n11, 58n14, 63, 71–74, 79, 83n62, 87, 90, 97–99, 105, 107, 113–114, 117, 121, 123
Satloff, Robert, 107
Sayigh, Yezid, 83n62
Shahrur, Muhammad, 54
Sharabi, Hisham, 63, 67, 71, 73–74
Shils, Edward, 24n32, 83n82
Sivan, Emmanuel, 81n30
Smith, Wilfred Cantwell, 18
Social Science Research Council (SSRC), 6, 9, 23n17, 67, 69, 91–94, 101n35, 109–110, 113, 116, 124
Soroush, Abdolkarim, 53
Speiser, E. A., *84*
Stanford University, 15, 77, 106
State Department *see* Department of State
Stein, Kenneth W., *39*
Sub-Committee on Oriental, Slavonic, East European, and African Studies (Hayter Committee), 12
Sultan Program in Arab Studies (Berkeley), 112

T

Temple University, 48–49
Tibawi, A. L., 53–54, 59n35
Title VI, 11–12, 26n67, 85, 87–88, 91–96, 100n8, 100n9, 104, 113, 116, 123–129. *See also* National Defense Education Act; Department of Education
Tucker, Judith, *20*, 91
Tufts University, 53

U

UCLA, 10, 12, 15, 23n17, 36–37, 90, 100n8
United States Congress, 6, 11, 85–87, 92–95, 128
United States Information Agency, 92–93
United States Institute of Peace (USIP), 97
University of Arizona, 1, 96
University of California at Berkeley *see* Berkeley
University of California at Los Angeles *see* UCLA
University of California at Santa Barbara, 113
University of Chicago, 10, 14, 48, 66–67
University of Michigan, 12, 23n17
University of Pennsylvania, 23n17
University of Utah, 10, 100n8
University of Washington, 10

V

Vatikiotis, P. J., *13, 18,* 38, 120
Voll, John, 50, 55, 95, 97

W

Washington Institute for Near East Policy, 106

Waterbury, John, *79*, 108–109, 115
Watt, W. Montgomery, 30
Wright, Robin, 52–53, 68

Y

Young, T. Cuyler, 100n8

Z

Ziadeh, Farhat, 10, *17*